THEMES
for early years

WINTER

JENNY MORRIS

THEMES
for early years

Author Jenny Morris
Editors Jane Bishop and Susan Howard
Assistant editor Lesley Sudlow
Series designer Lynne Joesbury
Designers Clare Brewer and Rachael Hammond
Illustrations Cathy Hughes
Cover Lynne Joesbury
Action Rhymes, Poems and Stories compiled by Jackie Andrews
Songs compiled by Peter Morrell

Designed using Adobe Pagemaker
Processed by Scholastic Ltd, Leamington Spa

Published by Scholastic Ltd, Villiers House, Clarendon Avenue, Leamington Spa, Warwickshire CV32 5PR

© 1999 Scholastic Ltd Text © 1999 Jenny Morris
1 2 3 4 5 6 7 8 9   9 0 1 2 3 4 5 6 7 8

The publishers gratefully acknowledge permission to reproduce the following copyright material:
Ann Bryant for 'The winter weather band' © 1999, Ann Bryant, previously unpublished; **Clive Barnwell** for 'Little footprints' and 'Bobble hat' © 1999, Clive Barnwell, previously unpublished; **Tracey Blance** for 'Log fire' © 1999, Tracey Blance, previously unpublished; **John Foster** for 'It's snowed' © 1999, John Foster, previously unpublished; **Barbara Garrad** for the use of 'Wrap up' © 1999, Barbara Garrad, previously unpublished; **Penny Kent** for 'Winter seeds' © 1999, Penny Kent, previously unpublished; **Jean Kenward** for 'Reindeer' © 1999, Jean Kenward, previously unpublished; **Karen King** for 'Bianca's winter coat' © 1999, Karen King, previously unpublished; **Johanne Levy** for 'A happy new year to you' © 1999, Johanne Levy, previously unpublished; **Frances Lincoln Limited** for 'The Snow Whale' from **The Snow Whale** by Caroline Pitcher © 1996, Caroline Pitcher (1996, Frances Lincoln). **Tony Mitton** for 'Robin rhyme', 'Snow stamping' and 'Hibernating hedgehog' © 1999, Tony Mitton, previously unpublished; **Peter Morrell** for 'Candlelight' © 1999, previously unpublished; **Sue Nicholls** for 'Snowflakes' © 1999, Sue Nicholls, previously unpublished; **Random UK Limited** for **The Winter Hedgehog** by Ann and Reg Cartwright © 1989, Ann and Reg Cartwright (1989, Random House Children's Books); **Pat Sweet** for 'Five friendly snowmen' © 1999, Pat Sweet, previously unpublished; **Ward Lock Educational Ltd** for 'Footprints in the snow' from **Knock on the Door** by Jan Betts © 1980, Jan Betts (1980, Ward Lock Educational Ltd); **Stevie Ann Wilde** for 'A puzzle – What am I?' © 1999, Stevie Ann Wilde, previously unpublished; **Brenda Williams** for 'I've made a star', 'My treasure', 'Winter weather', 'Anyone bored?' and 'Winter friend' © 1999, Brenda Williams, previously unpublished. Every effort has been made to trace copyright holders and the publishers apologize for any inadvertent omissions.

British Library Cataloguing-in-Publication Data A catalogue record for this book is available from the British Library.

ISBN 0-590-53898-5

The right of Jenny Morris to be identified as the Author of this work has been asserted by her in accordance with the Copyright, Designs and Patents Act 1988.

CONTENTS

INTRODUCTION

In the United Kingdom, towards the end of October, the clocks are put back one hour. This is officially referred to as 'The end of British summertime' and signals the beginning of winter. Many people groan at the hour change, they dislike the winter season with its short hours of daylight and cold weather. They view winter as a gloomy, sleepy time of year and they pile on extra layers of clothes, resigning themselves to getting through the winter months as quickly as possible. They long for the warmer, longer days of spring. Winter is the slow time of year when there is little visible plant growth and the pace of life slackens giving us time to be more leisurely.

Even young children are aware of these changes. They notice that the street lamps and car headlights are turned on while they are still out and about; they know that it is dark when they go to bed; they are told that they must wear coats when they go outside; they see that many trees are bare having dropped their autumn leaves onto the ground. Use this time of year to involve the children in investigating all the changes that winter brings.

AIMS

The winter season is not all doom and gloom, for there are many interesting things to do and see during this time. Young children would find the explanation of why we have different seasons far too difficult to understand, so this book does not study the way the Earth rotates on its axis and its relationship to the sun. Instead, it aims to cover aspects of winter which are relevant and interesting for children from three to six years. The activities in this book will promote language development and numeracy and enable children to compare the similarities and differences of winter to the other three seasons.

Chapter 1, 'Winter weather', shows weather conditions in this country to be both bleak and beautiful. It explains the dangers of winter when roads are icy or impassable because of snow drifts and contrasts the fun that can be had from sliding on ice or making snowmen and snowballs. Chapter 2, 'Clothes in winter', examines the type of clothes worn in the United Kingdom throughout November, December and January and encourages the children to compare them with clothes worn in other climates during the same months. Chapter 3, 'Winter at home', shows how people cope with the cold weather and how they spend their time during the longer dark hours. Chapter 4, 'Animals in winter', explores the ways in which different animals adapt to wintry conditions, how they protect themselves from the cold and yet ensure they have enough food. Chapter 5 demonstrates what happens to 'Plants in winter' — some die off, leaving their seeds behind to germinate in the warmer weather to come, others shrink back to their roots which remain hidden and protected in the earth. Chapter 6 is about 'Winter celebrations' — this is when people remember and give thanks for the past year, and think ahead to the brighter, warmer, longer days when nature wakes up and springs into life again.

The earth needs a quiet time, just like people do, and this book on winter can show children the value of slowing down, of relaxing physically and mentally and of having times of peace and calm to recharge their batteries.

HOW TO USE THIS BOOK

The activities in this book, although relevant to the winter season, do not depend on specific weather conditions which would make a straitjacket for topic planning. This applies especially to the activities in the chapter 'Winter weather'. The other chapters will benefit from being completed one at a time so that comparisons and similarities can be made. However, the chapter 'Winter celebrations' will be more meaningful if the activities are implemented as near as possible to the calendar dates. Whichever order is chosen, please remember that they are meant to be fun for everyone and to be enjoyed!

Most of the activities need very little preparation and use inexpensive non-specialist equipment. It is a good idea to check through the 'What you need' sections in the chapter 'Plants in winter', before the onset of winter, so that any necessary natural materials can be saved.

You will not need to spend precious time leafing through other books to find stories, poems and music which are appropriate to the winter topic because this book, like all the others in the series, contains a resources section with material specifically selected for the theme.

Wherever possible try to involve parents; not only are they a wonderful source of materials and equipment but their enthusiasm will help to foster the involvement of the children. Keep them well informed of what you are doing so that they can encourage and extend the children's learning and at the same time ask them to give you feedback on how the children are responding to what you are doing. This is an excellent way for you to assess how the children are progressing.

TOPIC WEB

On pages 8 and 9, the book's activities have been sorted into subject areas designated by the National Curriculum – English, Maths, Science, Music, Art, Design and Technology, RE, PE, History and Geography. The pages are photocopiable and can be pinned up and used as a reference so you know which subjects have been covered. They can also be used for future planning.

ACTIVITY PAGES

The book is divided into eight chapters, each relating to a different aspect of winter. The first six chapters have eight pages, each with an identical

format. There is a main activity which links the 'objectives' to one of the ten areas of the National Curriculum.

The 'group size' is merely an indication of the optimum number of children to be involved at any one time. Most group leaders will want to vary this according to the age of their children and the amount of help and space available.

Usually, the 'Preparation' for the main activity is minimal. However, a group leader may be able to give some of these tasks to the older and more able children who will probably take great pride in having this responsibility.

Any materials and equipment needed for the main activities are described in the 'What you need' section. Whenever something may be difficult to obtain, alternatives have been suggested. Tell the children what you will be doing and enlist their help to collect the items. This will help to increase their interest and excitement.

'What to do' takes you through the main activity stage by stage and this is often reinforced by diagrams and pictures. The 'Discussion' section which follows will hopefully be a dialogue between children and adults, and is not intended to be separated from 'What to do'. You may well be having your 'Discussion' prior to, during and after the activity.

The 'Follow-up activities' are cross-curricular and often extend the main activity. They vary in difficulty and some may be suitable for older children, while others may be more appropriate for the younger age range.

DISPLAYS

There are five different interactive winter displays in this chapter. It is hoped that you will assemble the displays using what is essentially the children's art, craft and written work. The results may fall short of exhibition standard but there is nothing more encouraging than for children to see their work on show and therefore valued. If care is taken with clear labelling the display can be used for reading and observation purposes.

ASSEMBLIES

The three winter assemblies in this chapter suggest ways in which children and adults can create and use sharing times. Although they focus on moral issues, there is no reason why a group leader

should not include some religious concepts relating to the different ethnic principles of the group. The children are encouraged to take part in role-plays and to reflect on their meaning.

RESOURCES

Stories, songs, poems and rhymes — all about winter — have been compiled for the convenience of a busy group leader. They can be photocopied and then read or sung in conjunction with specific activities or they can be used independently.

PHOTOCOPIABLE ACTIVITY SHEETS

There are eight activity or game sheets which can be photocopied and completed by the children, either to reinforce a specific main activity or used as part of the activity itself.

RECOMMENDED MATERIALS

This page lists picture and story books, music and songs, poems and rhymes, references, resources and information books which have been used in this book or can be used as additional 'Winter' theme material.

EXPRESSIVE ARTS

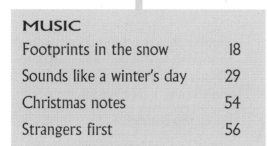

Planning towards the National Curriculum and the Scottish National guidelines 5–14

PREPARING FOR PRIMARY SCHOOL

THE NATIONAL CURRICULUM

To make sure that all children in England and Wales cover a wide range of subjects in state schools, the Government has introduced the National Curriculum. This means that when children start compulsory education at five years old, it is certain that they will be covering the same areas of the curriculum, for the same amount of time each week, as a child in any other state school, anywhere in the country.

The National Curriculum subjects are Mathematics, English, Science, Geography, History, Design and Technology, Physical Education, Religious Education, Art, Music and Information Technology. The Programme of Study gives guidance to teachers of what should be taught in each subject.

Children's progress is assessed in Year Two (when they are six or seven) by National Attainment Tests and by the teacher's personal judgement.

Although the National Curriculum does not involve pre-school children, it would seem wise to

give them a thorough grounding in the subjects which they will soon be meeting.

This book sets out to give just such a grounding based around the theme of winter. The children will be introduced to the concept of survival for people, animals and plants. They will have the opportunity to experiment on the effects of temperature changes and will be able to hear about the origins of some winter festivals. These activities and all the others, have clear learning objectives which link in to relevant National Curriculum subject areas and will provide children with a firm foundation for their further education. The Topic web on pages 8 and 9 shows the division of subject areas and activities.

THE SCOTTISH NATIONAL GUIDELINES 5–14

In Scotland, there are National Guidelines for schools on what should be taught to children between the ages of five and fourteen.

These National Guidelines are divided into six main curriculum areas: English Language, Mathematics, Environmental Studies, Expressive Arts, Religious and Moral Education, and Personal and Social Development.

Within these main areas further subjects are found, for example 'Expressive Arts' includes Art and Design, Drama, Music and PE. Strands are also identified within each subject, for example Maths includes problem-solving and enquiry, and shape, position and movement.

Most nurseries and playgroups will find that the experiences which they are offering to children will be laying a good foundation for this curriculum. This book provides activities which have been specially written to prepare for many aspects of it and they will also fit well into the pre-school curriculum guidelines issued by local authorities throughout Scotland.

To help with your planning, the individual activities have been allocated to separate areas of the curriculum on the Topic web on pages 8 and 9. The children's personal and social development is an ongoing theme that is incorporated throughout the activities in the book.

CHAPTER 1
WINTER WEATHER

British winters bring cold weather such as frost, fog, ice, hailstones and snow. This chapter looks at signs of these different weather conditions represented by activities such as cake and soup making, melting ice and singing about footprints in the snow.

SIGNS OF WINTER

Objectives

English — To be aware that two letters can blend to make one sound and to play a matching game.

Group size

Four children.

What you need

A large piece of card and a marker pen, three copies of photocopiable page 88 on thin card, a pair of scissors.

Preparation

Copy photocopiable page 88 onto three pieces of card. Cut up two copies of the sheet to make two matching sets of picture cards.

cards and turn them over. If the pictures match each other, the pair can be kept and the child can have another go. If they don't match, the cards should be faced down again, ready for the next child to try and find a matching pair.

Discussion

The six pictures on the photocopiable sheet are all seen in winter when the weather in our country is cold and we need to keep ourselves warm. We wear woolly scarves to keep our necks warm and some people who have fireplaces make a fire inside their house. How does the smoke leave the house? (Through a chimney.) What kind of weather do we need to be able to ski, sledge and to make snowmen?

What to do

Show the children the uncut photocopiable sheet and talk about the pictures of skis, smoke, sledge, snowman, skates and scarf. Read the name of each item as you run your finger under the word. See if anyone notices that all the words begin with the same letter 's'. Say each word carefully to highlight that although they all begin with 's', the beginnings of the words sound different.

On the large card, write the first two letters of each word in turn and let the children see you circle the first two letters together, explaining that they can make one sound. Lay the picture cards face down on a table and ask a child to pick two

Follow-up activities

✧ Talk about the dangers of fires. Point out to the children that they should never use or play with matches and lighters.
✧ Do any of the children have first or second names that begin with a two letter blend?
✧ Which animals names begin with 's' blends? (Skunk, skate (fish), slug, snake, snail, swan, sheep.)
✧ Explain that when you want children to be quiet you say 'sh' and put you finger up against your lips, 'sh' is another 's' blend.
✧ Move as if you were skiing, sledging or skating.
✧ Sing the song 'Five friendly snowmen' on page 81 and read the story 'The snow whale' on page 76.

FROSTED MUNCHIES

Objectives

Design and Technology – To select suitable tools and gather ingredients to make individual cakes.

Group size

Three children.

What you need

A heat source, a saucepan, kitchen scales, a hammer, four teaspoons, a wooden spoon, a tablespoon, a wad of newspaper, aprons/overalls, individual bun cases, a handful of plain cornflakes (for demonstration only). Ingredients (quantities given will make about 18 cakes): a packet of sugar-coated cornflakes (375g), 100g marshmallows, 100g margarine, 100g slab of toffee (from supermarkets or sweet shops), one tablespoon of golden syrup.

What to do

Ask the children to wash their hands thoroughly before handling the food. As this is a very sticky recipe it would be wise for the children to wear overalls! Show them the two types of cornflakes and note the difference.

Let each child pick out five marshmallows and put them into the saucepan. Weigh the margarine and add this to the pan along with the syrup. Ask the children to select a suitable tool for breaking up the toffee and then let them smash the slab (still in its wrapper) onto the wad of newspaper on the floor. Add the toffee pieces to the pan and stir everything over a very gentle heat with the wooden spoon – do not let it boil.

When the ingredients have melted and thickened, remove the pan from the heat and add enough sugar-coated cornflakes to use up all the mixture. Stir well to ensure all the flakes are coated. Spoon the 'Frosted munchies' into the paper cases and leave to set for about an hour. If the mixture starts to set too soon, reheat it for a moment.

Discussion

When the weather is very cold the moisture in the air freezes and leaves a layer of white frost over the ground outside and feathery patterns on the window panes. Which of the two types of cornflakes looked as if they had been covered with a layer of frost? What happens to frost when the sun shines? Can anyone describe what a frosty spider's web looks like?

Follow-up activities

✧ Scrape some frosted ice off the sides of a freezer and look at it through a magnifying glass. The frosty little bobbles you can see look the same as ground frost.
✧ Shake some icing sugar through a sieve onto a table top and it will look as if it has been covered in frost.
✧ Paint the upper side of broken twigs with white paint to look as if they have been out in the frost.
✧ Some glass windows are described as frosted – can you see through them?

MELTING ICE

Objective

Science – To find out whether ice will melt more quickly when salt is added.

Group size

Whole group.

What you need

A tray of ice cubes, two shallow bowls, salt and a teaspoon, labelling card, pencil.

Preparation

Freeze some water into ice cubes.

What to do

Ask the children to listen carefully as you twist the ice cubes out of their tray. Let them handle the cubes and slide them across a table top.

Put one ice cube into each of the bowls and sprinkle a teaspoon of salt onto one of the cubes. Prepare a label for each bowl writing 'with salt', 'without salt' or ask an able child to do this. Leave the bowls where they can be observed easily by the children and ask them to tell you when they notice any changes.

When one of the cubes has completely melted, look at the other cube and note any differences. The salted cube will have melted first because when salt mixes with ice it makes salty water. Salt water needs to be much colder than plain water to freeze.

Discussion

What type of sound did the ice cubes make when they were twisted out of their tray? (Cracking, creaking.) Were the ice cubes hard or soft? Why could they slide so easily across the table? (They were slippery.) Which of the ice cubes melted faster? In winter when it is very cold, water can freeze into hard ice. This can make the ground treacherous for people or cars to move over, but if salt is

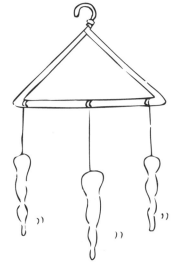

sprinkled onto it, the ice will melt faster. Sometimes sand and grit are sprinkled onto ice instead of salt and this helps cars and people's feet to grip the ice.

Follow-up activities

✧ Leave the water in both the bowls to evaporate. Then look through a magnifying glass and see the crystals that the salt has left in one of the bowls.
✧ Experiment with other things to melt ice; try hot water, sugar or sand.
✧ Freeze water in a large shallow baking tray. Slide a toy car across the ice. Now sprinkle some sand on the surface and try to slide the car again.
✧ Ask the children to look out for salt, sand or grit bins near busy road junctions.
✧ What sound would you hear if you were travelling in a car on a road that had been gritted?
✧ Dripping water can freeze into icicles. Cut large narrow pointed shapes out of washed tin foil food containers. Suspend these shapes from a coat-hanger to make an attractive icicle mobile.

A PEA SOUP

Objectives

Geography – To be aware of our environment, and to make some pea soup.

Group size

Four children

What you need

A source of heat for cooking, a saucepan, a 1 litre measuring jug, kitchen scales, a pair of scissors for each child, a wooden spoon, a sharp knife (for adults only) and a chopping board, an empty glass and a glass of water. Ingredients: a bunch of spring onions (100g), 50g of butter or margarine, a 500g packet of green split peas, 1.2 litres of water, 2 vegetable stock cubes, salt and pepper.

Preparation

Soak 225g of the peas in 1.2 litres of water overnight. Clean the onions and prepare them ready for cutting.

What to do

Show the children the glass of water and ask them to look through it. Explain to them that it is as clear to look through as is the air. Ask the children to use the scissors and cut the spring onions into

small rings. Melt the butter in the saucepan, add the onions and cover them until they have softened. Add the soaked peas and water and crumble in the stock cubes. Bring it all to the boil and simmer for approximately two hours until the peas are soft enough to disintegrate.

Stir the cooked soup in front of the children and ask them where the peas have gone. Pour some soup into a glass and place it next to the glass of water. Can the children see clearly through the glass of pea soup?

Discussion

When the weather is foggy it seems like there are clouds on the ground which cling to everything. Factories used to burn coal and on foggy days the smoke mixed with the fog and made a thick yellow smog which people often called 'pea soup'. This air was very dirty for people to breathe, so factories now use cleaner fuel such as electricity and nuclear fuel. When you compared the glass of clear water to the glass of pea soup, which was easier to see through? Looking through water is like looking through clean air. Trying to see through pea soup is like trying to see through smog!

Follow-up activities

✧ Try wearing a mask which decorators or builders wear to filter the air you breathe.
✧ Paint a picture of a car and let the children rub yellow chalk all over it to look like smog.
✧ Explain that split peas are broken or split into two pieces. Show them the long break in a split pin or a split in the seam of some clothing.
✧ Say the poem 'Winter weather' on page 68.

ROLLING ALONG

Objectives

PE – To practise moving together and to play a game of touch.

Group size

Not more than twelve children.

What you need

25g of self-raising flour (*not* plain flour), approximately 150ml of water, a mixing bowl and fork, flour in a shaker (you can make one using a cream carton with holes pierced in its lid, secured with sticky tape), a dark coloured tray or a chopping board.

Preparation

Mix together the flour and water to make a dough. Knead it ready for your demonstration.

What to do

Sprinkle the tray with flour and roll a small ball of dough over it so that the children can see how the dough-ball will 'pick up' the sprinkled flour. Move the ball around the tray to show how the flour sticks to the dough. Let the children try this out for themselves. (Moisten the dough slightly if it becomes too dry.)

Explain that you want them to play a game of sticking together. Ask the children to space out as much as they can and then move slowly round the room with their arms outstretched. When they brush against another child they can link arms together. They should continue 'rolling' around until they touch another child or group of children. Eventually all the children should be 'stuck' together just like a giant snowball. It may be easier to start this game with only a few children and to gradually let more children join in.

Discussion

Sometimes in winter when it is very cold little drops of water freeze into snowflakes. These fall from the clouds and cover everything with snow. What can you make if you squeeze snow together in-between your two hands? If this snowball is rolled over snowy ground it will pick up more snow just like the dough-ball picked up flour. What will happen to the little snowball as it picks up more and more snow? Can anything be made with a big snowball? A snowman can have a smaller snowball for its head.

Follow-up activities

✧ Scrape some frozen ice from the sides of a kitchen freezer and show the children how this can be squeezed into a ball.
✧ Make enough of the flour dough for each child to make their own snowballs or snowman. Add slivers of carrot and some currants for face features. Bake the 'snowmen' in the oven for approximately ten minutes.
✧ Let the children practise rolling a plastic or rubber ball across the floor to a partner.
✧ Read the poem 'Winter friend' on page 67.

LACY FLAKES

Objectives

Design and Technology – To fold and cut paper to make a decorative snowflake shape.

Group size

Four children.

What you need

A picture of snowflakes, a pair of scissors and one white paper circle (measuring 20cm diameter) for each child, a plate approximately 20cm, a pencil and sharp pair of scissors, some Blu-Tack, a cake made from flaky pastry (such as a vanilla slice), a pointed knife (for adults only).

Preparation

Draw round the plate onto the white paper and cut out four circles.

What to do

Remove the top piece of pastry from the vanilla slice and show the children how your knife can separate the pastry into flakes. Explain that you want the children to make a paper snowflake each. Give them a circle each and ask them to fold it in half. Then show them how to fold it into thirds:

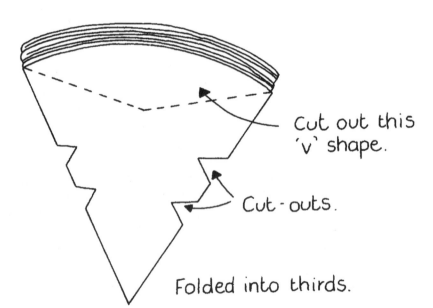

Cut out this 'v' shape.

Cut-outs.

Folded into thirds.

Pencil a 'V' shape on the top layer of the folded paper and ask the children to cut this out. Now ask them to make cut-outs along the two sides. They will need to actually cut away some paper not just make cuts.

When the children have finished cutting, ask them to open up their folded paper. Stick the snowflakes on the window with Blu-Tack and look carefully at the patterns.

Discussion

The pastry consisted of flat, thin, pieces. How would you describe a snowflake? How many points does it have? (Snowflakes always have six points which are arranged an equal distance apart from each other – this is called symmetrical.) No snowflakes ever have exactly the same pattern. What other things are made in flakes? (Cornflakes, chocolate flakes, soap flakes.)

Follow-up activities

✧ Snowflakes are very light and float down from the sky. Ask the children to move round the room as if they were floating snowflakes.
✧ A Star of David is another six pointed shape. A blue Star of David is the Jewish symbol on the flag of Israel. Make a Star of David by sticking one triangle over another.
✧ Look through a kaleidoscope and see some more symmetrical patterns.
✧ Use fluted baking bun cases to cut small paper snowflakes. Stick them over a large sheet of black paper to make a wall picture.
✧ Say the tongue twister 'Five flakes floated over Farmer Fred's field'.
✧ Sing the song 'Snowflakes' on page 81 and read the poem 'Snow stamping' on page 69 with the children.

ICE BALLS

Objectives

Science – To discover how water changes when it is frozen and to make some 'hailstones'.

Group size

Four children.

What you need

A jug of water and four beakers, a large packet of Plasticine, four thick pencils of 1cm diameter, a shallow baking tray, a medicine dropper (from a chemist), paper towels, a small screwdriver, access to a freezer or ice box.

What to do

Give each child a tangerine-sized piece of Plasticine and ask them to hold it in both hands to warm it. Show them how to press and pat it into a flat shape approximately 1cm thick. Give a pencil to each child and ask them to press the flat end into the Plasticine to make five hollows. Ensure that they do not press right through the Plasticine which would make a hole.

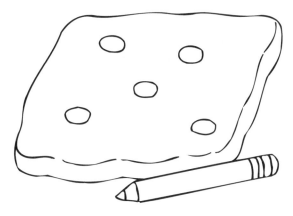

Put the Plasticine moulds onto the baking tray. Let each child pour some water from the jug into a beaker and then ask them to take turns using the medicine dropper to fill up all the hollows in their mould with water. Mop up any spills with paper towels. Place the baking tray carefully in the freezer and leave for an hour or until the water has frozen. Let the children touch the frozen water before you ease the balls out of the Plasticine using the tip of the screwdriver.

Discussion

How had the water changed after it had been in the freezer? Can hard water (ice) be poured from a jug? Did you notice that the top of each ice ball had become rounded and was peeping up out of the mould? (Water expands when it freezes.) In winter frozen drops of water form in thunderclouds and become so heavy that they fall to the ground as hailstones. Sometimes hailstones are so hard that when they hit the ground they make a lot of noise and bounce back into the air. Very big hailstones can damage the plants in the garden.

Follow-up activities

✧ Drop some pebbles onto a tambourine or the lid of a polythene box. This is the type of sound that large hailstones can make.
✧ Hailstones can bounce. Practise bouncing a large beach ball with the flat of your hand.
✧ Use dried white beans that look like hailstones and arrange them into number patterns.
✧ Hailstones are white – think of as many white things as you can.
✧ Talk about the differences between a snowflake and a hailstone.
✧ Sing the song 'The winter weather band' on page 80 together.

FOOTPRINTS IN THE SNOW

Objectives

Music – To sing a song about snow and to make the appropriate animal actions.

Group size

The whole group.

What you need

A copy of the music and words to the song 'Footprints in the snow' on page 86, a picture of a sparrow, a pigeon, a cat, a squirrel and a horse.

What to do

Show the pictures to the children. Explain that when you show each picture you want them to move in a certain way. Ask them to hop when they see the picture of the sparrow, walk around themselves when they see the pigeon picture, spring forward when they see the cat, form their arm into a wavy tail when they see the squirrel and pretend to hold onto horses' reins when they see the picture of the horse.

Sing the song with the children several times until they are familiar with the words. Ask them to form a big circle. Sing the song together and give the children time after each verse to carry out the action which has just been described in the song. Use your pictures as prompts.

Discussion

When snow has fallen thickly overnight, the next morning everywhere looks as if it has been covered in a soft white blanket. If you look very carefully you might see little marks where different creatures have left their footprints. Creatures cannot find food easily when snow has covered the ground and all the plants.

Which of the animals in the song would leave the smallest footprints and which animal would leave the biggest?

Follow-up activities

✧ Give each child a copy of photocopiable page 89 and ask them to match the footprints to the different animals.
✧ Dip a toy car and a dressmaker's tracing wheel into black paint and roll them across a sheet of white paper to look like bicycle and car tracks in the snow.
✧ If you have a heavy fall of snow, go and walk in it and look at the impression your shoes or wellies have made. Stamp your name out in the snow.
✧ Sing the songs 'Footprints in the snow' on page 86, and 'Little footprints' on page 82.
✧ Birds need to be fed in very cold weather. Make breadcrumbs by rolling pieces of bread between your hands, then scatter them outside.

CHAPTER 2
CLOTHES IN WINTER

The special clothes we wear during the winter are to cope with varying weather conditions. In this chapter, there are activities to find out which clothes will keep us warm, which will keep us dry, which material is suitable for warming people in an emergency and how to care for clothes which are not warm enough for winter wear.

NECK AND NECK

Objective

Mathematics – To investigate the different shapes and lengths of scarves.

Group size

Whole group.

What you need

A selection of scarves of different shapes, sizes and patterns, including at least one square scarf and one long one.

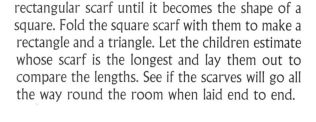

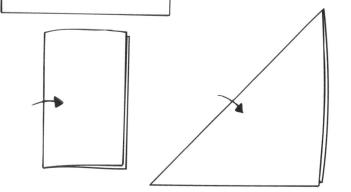

Preparation

Ask the children to each bring in a scarf from home and bring one in yourself.

What to do

Wear your scarf and ask the children to wear theirs. Check to see whether they can name the shapes of the scarves (square, rectangle, triangle). Show the children how to trace a finger all along the outside edge of their scarf and then to touch each of its corners.

Ask them to fold their scarf in half (by matching corners) and to see whether this alters the shape (not size) of the scarf. Help them to fold a rectangular scarf until it becomes the shape of a square. Fold the square scarf with them to make a rectangle and a triangle. Let the children estimate whose scarf is the longest and lay them out to compare the lengths. See if the scarves will go all the way round the room when laid end to end.

Discussion

One of the ways in which we can keep warmer in winter is to wear a scarf. How did the children decide how and where to wear their scarves? Discuss the different places you can wear a scarf and that this may depend on the shape and size of the scarf or on family preferences. Talk about the different patterns and colours on the scarves and how some represent schools or football teams.

Follow-up activities

✧ Randomly colour horizontal stripes on sheets of white A4 paper. Stick all the sheets together to make a long, striped scarf and fix it round the walls of your room. Decorate the ends with pieces of wool to make a fringe.
✧ Find other uses for a scarf such as a bandage, a doll's blanket, a cushion or a teddy's hammock.
✧ Cut out a narrow strip of material and use it for a doll's scarf.
✧ Point out that the plural of scarf is scarves, of calf is calves, and of leaf is leaves.
✧ Share the poem 'Wrap up' on page 67.
✧ Make a patchwork quilt by arranging some scarves together.

MY MUFF

Objectives

History – To find out how people in the past kept their hands warm and to make a muff.

Group size

Four children.

What you need

A picture of a muff (in *Clothes and Fashion Long Ago* by Felicity Brooks (Usborne Explainers) or see the Adults' Encyclopaedia Britannica for a reference). Four sheets of thin A4 card, sticky tape, three saucers with brightly coloured paint in, PVA adhesive and spreaders, enough bubble wrap to line each card (optional), sharp scissors (for adults only), an A4-sized piece of fake fur fabric, needle and thread.

Preparation

Wrap the fake fur over and tack it along the short edge to make a muff with the fur on the inside. Mix the paints. Cut the bubble wrap into four pieces each measuring 6cm short of A4 size.

What to do

Show the children the pictures of a muff and then show them the one you have made, letting them take turns to put their hands in it. Explain that you want them to make a pretend muff, like people in the past used to wear.

Give each child a sheet of card and show them how to dip their finger into a saucer of paint and make a finger print pattern all over the card. When the paint on the card is dry, stick a bubble-wrap lining for warmth onto the blank side, leaving a 3cm margin at each end of the card. Help the children to roll their card into a tube with the painted pattern on the outside. Use sticky tape to secure the tube down the centre leaving both ends open. Let the children wear their muffs.

Discussion

One of the ways that people used to keep their hands warm during winter was to put them inside a tube of soft warm fabric called a muff. Ladies' muffs often matched the clothes they wore. What do we use to keep our hands warm today? (Gloves or mittens.) How are muffs different from gloves? (You need two gloves (a pair) but only one muff.) Some muffs were used to carry money and handkerchiefs as well as to keep hands warm. How do we carry money? (Purses, wallets or pockets.) Could you ride a bike while you were wearing a muff? What is a good way to prevent you losing your gloves? (Attach them to string/elastic inside your coat.)

Follow-up activities

✧ Cut a cardboard tube open along its length and ask the children what shape it has made now that it is flat. (A rectangle.)
✧ Compare a pair of gloves and a pair of mittens. Count the fingers and thumbs.
✧ Say the nursery rhyme together 'Three Little Kittens They Lost Their Mittens'.

WET AND DRIP

Objective

Science – To find out which clothes will keep us dry when it's raining.

Group size

Four children.

What you need

Clothing made of different fabrics such as a waxed jacket, an anorak, a PVC raincoat, a denim jacket, a plastic apron, a woollen sweater, a cotton T-shirt, a towelling wrap, a pair of nylon tights, a pair of slippers, a pair of wellingtons, a woolly bobble hat, a plastic rain hat. A long handled sweeping brush, two chairs, clothes hangers, four empty plastic drink bottles, a craft knife (for adults only), a jug of water, four children's thick paintbrushes — perfectly clean, lots of newspaper.

Preparation

Make a clothes rack at child height by supporting the broom handle between two chairs. Cut the plastic water bottles in half and invert the tops back into the bases then pour some water into each of these pots.

What to do

Let the children handle the clothes collection and ask them to name each item and tell you on which part of the body it is worn. Ask them to help you put the clothes onto hangers and hang them on the rack.

Spread thick layers of newspaper under the rack of clothes and onto the seats of the two chairs. Place the slippers and wellingtons on the chair seats. Give each child a water pot and paintbrush and ask them to 'paint' water onto the clothes as if it were raining. Encourage them to notice what happens to the water. Ask them to feel inside the clothes to see if they are wet.

Discussion

What happened to the water that was painted onto the clothes? The clothes which the water dripped off are called waterproof. Did the clothes which 'held' the water (absorbed) feel wet inside? Which of the clothes would be suitable to wear in wet, winter weather? Why are some babies' bibs and children's overalls made from waterproof material?

Follow-up activities

✧ Open up an umbrella, put it on newspaper on the floor and let the children stand round and 'paint' the outside with water. Would an umbrella keep you wet or dry?
✧ Put a piece of sheep's wool into water, feel to see if it is wet then discuss other animal skins.
✧ Write your name on a sheet of paper with a wax crayon or candle. Paint a coloured wash over it and observe the waxed area. Compare the waxed paper to a waxed coat.
✧ Weigh a piece of dry sponge, wet it and then weigh it again. Why is the wet sponge heavier?

PICK A HAT

Objective

PE – To play a team game using winter hats.

Group size

Six children.

What you need

A piece of white chalk, two buckets, at least eight winter hats such as a woolly bobble hat, a baby's bonnet, a beret, a trilby, a sou'wester or rain hat, a wind protector with ear flaps, a flat cap, a balaclava.

Preparation

Make two rows of five chalk crosses on the floor at one metre intervals to position the hats and buckets.

What to do

Let the children handle the hats then talk about who would wear them and in which type of weather. Explain that you are going to play a game with the hats.

Place the buckets and hats on top of the chalk crosses in two rows.

Divide the children into two groups of three to stand in a line behind each bucket. Ask the first child in each line to run and pick up the first hat and return it to their bucket. Then to run to the second hat and do the same and then to the third hat. When all the hats have been picked up, the next child in the line should

replace all the hats, one at a time in the same fashion. The third child should pick them all up again. Which group of children finished first?

Discussion

Hats are worn for many different reasons but thick or waterproof hats are usually worn to keep people warm and dry.

People can lose more heat through their head than from any other part of their body. This is why a newborn baby in an incubator often wears a hat. Point out the broad flap at the back of the sou'wester which was originally designed to keep the rain off a fisherman's neck. In which kind of weather would you need to wear a hat with ear flaps? (Very windy.) A balaclava is a type of helmet that used to be worn by soldiers in extremely cold weather.

Follow-up activities

◇ Talk about other reasons why hats are worn: yarmulkes (skull caps) and turbans are worn for religious purposes, helmets and hard hats are worn for protection, caps and boaters can be part of a school uniform and some hats are worn just to look smart!

◇ Use sequin strips and pieces of shiny coloured paper to decorate a strip of card measuring 50cm × 6cm. Secure it to make a hat band for a crown.

◇ How many words can you think of which rhyme with hat. (At, bat, cat, fat, mat, gnat, pat, rat, sat, tat, vat.)

◇ Pile all the hats up on top of each other without letting them fall over.

◇ Sing the song 'Bobble hat' on page 83.

SHINY SURVIVAL

Objectives

Design and Technology – To design and make a survival blanket for a teddy.

Group size

Six children.

What you need

A roll of kitchen foil, two small potatoes (the same size), a plate, a pan of water and a heat source. An emergency foil blanket (obtainable from a camping shop), a pair of scissors (for adult use only), a small doll or soft toy for each child.

Preparation

Immediately before this activity, boil or microwave the two small potatoes and place them well away from the children.

What to do

Test that the potatoes are cool enough for the children to be able to feel the heat without burning their fingers. Wrap up one potato in a piece of silver foil. Place the wrapped and unwrapped potatoes on the plate. Allow the children to keep testing the heat of the unwrapped potato until it feels cool. Open up the foil and compare the heat of both potatoes.

Show the children the emergency foil blanket and tell them that you want them to make one for a small doll of their choice. Unroll the kitchen foil and ask each child to tell you how much they need to make a blanket for their doll. Cut the foil for them to wrap round their doll to keep it warm. If necessary remind the children that their 'person' needs to see and breathe!

Discussion

Which potato kept the warmest? A silver foil wrap can trap heat. Sometimes during winter when people go walking in the hills, snow can fall so heavily that they can't find their way home. What could they carry with them for extra warmth? An emergency blanket made from foil can stop people losing too much heat too quickly. Why wouldn't climbers carry a woollen blanket? (Too heavy.) Very tiny new babies are sometimes wrapped in a foil blanket to stop them losing heat.

Follow-up activities

✧ Wrap an ice cube in foil and leave it on a plate next to an unwrapped ice cube. Which cube melts first? A foil parcel can trap heat or cold inside.
✧ Anchor a coin to a table top with a piece of Blu-Tack. Place a piece of foil over the coin and use a flattened finger-tip to make a rubbing.
✧ Make a collection of shiny things such as silver foil and foil food containers, mirrors and spoons. Shine a torch on them and see which is the shiniest.
✧ Warm your hands by cupping them round your mouth and breathe out slowly until you feel the warmth on them.

SHORTS AND LONGS

Objective

Geography – To be aware that during the cold winter in the United Kingdom the weather is hot in other parts of the world.

Group size

Six children.

What you need

A collection of summer clothes (shorts, a cotton T-shirt, short cotton socks, a bathing costume, trunks, sun-dress, sun-hat, sandals) and winter clothes (long trousers, boots, wellingtons, gloves, a hat, a scarf, a vest, tights, a woollen pullover). A bag big enough to hold the clothes, a globe or map of the world, two pieces of A4 white card, a red and a blue marker pen.

Preparation

Write the word 'hot' in large red lettering on one of the cards and the word 'cold' in large blue lettering on the other card. Pile the 'summer' and 'winter' clothes separately.

What to do

Ask the children to describe the clothes they are wearing today and then to name all the cold weather clothes which you have collected. Show the children the position of the United Kingdom on the globe or the map and then point to the line running horizontally across the middle (the Equator). Explain that children who live near this middle area have hot weather all year round. Now encourage your group to name the hot weather clothes you have gathered. Explain that these are the type of clothes which the children in hot climates might be wearing while we are wearing winter clothes.

Put the prepared 'hot' and 'cold' cards on the floor a little way apart. Mix up all the winter and summer clothes and put them into the bag. Let the children take turns to select an item from the bag, name it and then sort it into either the 'hot' or 'cold' pile.

Discussion

During the cold winter months people who live in the United Kingdom need to dress in very warm clothes. Which clothes do people in hotter climates wear at this time of year? What kind of food do people eat during cold weather? (Soups, porridge, hot stews and puddings.) What kind of food do people eat during hot weather? (Ice-cream, fruit, salads.) Children in hot countries can play outside all year while we have to stay indoors in winter to keep warm.

Follow-up activities

✧ Give each child a copy of photocopiable page 90 and ask them to colour in red all the clothes which are worn in hot weather, and to colour in blue the cold weather clothes.
✧ Hot is the opposite of cold, think of some other opposite words.
✧ Find the coldest places in the world at the two poles, which are at the top and bottom of the globe or map, with the children.

WARM, WARMER, WARMEST

Objective

English – To practise describing things by comparison.

Group size

Work with three children at a time.

What you need

A sweater and coat for each child. Three dolls and a selection of dolls' clothes which will fit them (babies clothes might be suitable for big dolls).

Preparation

Take all the clothes off the dolls.

What to do

Discuss with the children how we keep ourselves warm in winter. If the children are wearing cardigans or sweaters, ask them to take them off for a minute. Do you still feel warm? Ask them to put their sweaters back on again. Do you feel warmer? Now ask them to put their coats on. Does this make you feel the warmest?

Give the children a doll each and tell them that the dolls are going to get dressed for the day. Ask one child to dress their doll in underwear and top clothes only, another child to dress his doll in underwear, top clothes and a sweater and the third child to dress her doll in underwear, top clothes, sweater and a coat. Arrange the dolls in a row and ask the children which doll they think is warm, which is warmer and which is the warmest. How can

you tell? Rearrange the dolls and see if the children can still compare the warmth of the dolls.

Discussion

When we dress ourselves in winter we choose warm clothes. What do we do if we aren't warm enough? By wearing an extra layer of clothes we can make ourselves warmer. Although thick clothes are warmer than thin clothes, the way to be the warmest of all is to wear clothes in layers. Each layer of clothing traps warm air in between and the more layers of trapped air the warmer we are. Why do duvets keep us so warm in bed? (They trap air in between their fibres or feathers.)

Follow-up activities

✧ Take some clothes off the dolls and guess which one is cold, which is colder than the others and which is the coldest.
✧ Use the dressing up clothes to see how many layers of clothes you can fit on all together. Who is hot, who is hotter and who is the hottest?
✧ Wrap some squeezy bottles in 'coats' of different fabrics such as towelling, fur fabric, wool and cotton. Fill the bottles with hot water and see which fabric keeps the bottle hottest.
✧ Compare some toy cars. Which is big, bigger and biggest? Which is small, smaller and smallest?
✧ Read the story 'Bianca's winter coat' on page 78.

BOXED UP

Objectives

RE – To pack clothes away and to see the importance of looking after our things.

Group size

Four children.

What you need

A collection of summer clothes of different textures such as cotton, linen, nylon, wool, polyester, towelling, acrylic and at least one pair of summer shoes. A box in which to pack the clothes. A plastic carrier bag for each pair of shoes.

Preparation

On the night before carrying out this activity, crumple up an item of cotton clothing so that it will look really creased.

What to do

Name and examine all the summer clothes and discuss their thickness, texture, pattern and use. Talk about whether they will be needed during the winter months, and if there will be enough room in the cupboards and drawers for summer and winter clothes to be kept together. Ask for suggestions of how you might solve the problem.

Tell the children that you want them to pack the summer clothes away in a box until they will be needed again. Show them the crumpled item and explain that unless clothes are folded or hung up carefully, they will end up being very creased. Ask the children how can they prevent the shoes from making the other clothes dirty. Show the children how to wrap the shoes in the carrier bags and place them in the bottom of the box first.

Discussion

We need to take care of all the things we have, just like our parents and teachers show care. Because we wear different clothes in winter than we do in summer, it is sensible to pack away the clothes which are not needed. What will happen if we don't fold the clothes carefully? Some clothes crease much more than others. When the warmer weather arrives what will we do with the winter clothes? (Pack them away.) Sometimes children cannot fit into the clothes which have been packed away during the winter, why is this? (They have grown!)

Follow-up activities

✧ Push some clothes into a bag without folding them. Next day, see which have become creased.
✧ Pack some clothes into a small case and pretend you are ready to go away on holiday.
✧ Assemble a collection of different sized boxes and fit them into each other, or arrange them in order of size starting with either the smallest box or the largest.
✧ Play with a box car. Cut out a large oval shape from the bottom of a deep fruit box then fix two paper plates to each side with split pins. Fix two foil plates onto the front of the box for headlights.

CHAPTER 3
WINTER AT HOME

Winter is a time for staying indoors and sheltering from the cold weather. This chapter explains how people in the past warmed their houses and how we can measure temperatures. It deals with the problems of being snowed in and suggests ways of how to spend time playing indoor games or performing exercises to keep warm.

SOOTY CHIMNEYS

Objectives

History – To find out about the life of children in the past.

Group size

Four children.

What you need

A picture of a house with a chimney, a packet of charcoal (obtainable from an art or stationery shop), a sheet of A4 white paper for each child, a ruler, a thick black pen, a damp cloth.

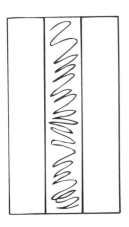

Preparation

Draw two thick black lines down the length of each piece of white paper so that there will be a tall chimney down the middle measuring 7cm wide.

What to do

Show the children the picture of the house and point out where the chimney is. Give each child a piece of paper and point out the tall chimney drawn on it. Open the packet of charcoal and ask the children to choose a piece each and to handle it gently. Explain that chimneys take the smoke away from fires then ask them to rub their piece of charcoal 'inside' the paper chimney so that it will be all sooty like the inside of a real chimney.

Afterwards, ask the children to wipe their hands on the damp cloth or you will have lots of sooty marks around your room!

Discussion

In the past when there was no electricity or central heating, people had to burn fires in their homes to keep themselves warm during the cold winter weather. When a fire burns it makes smoke which can escape up a chimney. This smoke leaves black powdery soot sticking to the sides of the chimney. Small children used to be sent up chimneys carrying a brush to sweep away all the soot. Would this be a clean or a dirty job? Was handling the charcoal clean or dirty? What did the charcoal feel like? (Light and fragile.) It is made from burnt out logs or coal. Do you have barbecues at home? What do your parents use to make the fire? Do any of your houses have open fireplaces where you burn coal and logs?

Follow-up activities

✧ Talk about the danger of fire and warn the children that they must stand well back from bonfires and barbecues.
✧ Read the first two pages of *Water Babies* by Charles Kingsley (Penguin) about a chimney sweep called Tom.
✧ Say this tongue-twister: 'Six sooty sweeps swept several smoky chimneys'.
✧ Build a tall chimney using construction toys.
✧ Squeeze through a small space, such as the legs of a chair, to see what squeezing up a chimney would have been like.
✧ Read the poem 'Log fire' on page 71.

TAKING TEMPERATURES

Objectives

Mathematics – To measure and record different water temperatures.

Group size

Two children.

What you need

A simple Celsius thermometer, two glass tumblers, a source of cold and hot tap water (not boiling), three ice cubes, two copies of photocopiable page 91, two red pencil crayons.

Preparation

Make some ice cubes the day before this activity.

What to do

Show the children the thermometer, point out where the numbers are and the narrow tube with a bulb at its base. Ask the children what colour liquid is in the tube. Explain to them that a thermometer can tell us if water, air or our bodies are hot or cold.

Pour hot water into one glass tumbler and a mixture of ice cubes and cold water into the other and let the children feel the outside of both glasses. Make sure that both children can see the narrow thermometer tube and then place the thermometer into the glass of hot water. What happens to the red liquid? Now put the thermometer in the icy water and watch again what happens to the red liquid. Repeat this several times so the children can see the red liquid going up or down and know which glass produces which result.

Give the children a red crayon and a copy of photocopiable sheet 91 each. Compare the sheet to the real thermometer. Repeat the experiments giving the children time in-between to colour the paper tube up to the appropriate level as shown on the thermometer.

Discussion

Where did the red liquid settle in the thermometer in each glass of water? Although we know that winter weather is cold, on some days it is colder than others. If we look at where the red level is on a thermometer each morning we will know if we need to put on extra clothes for the day. Will this be when the red line on the thermometer is high or low?

Follow-up activities

✧ Measure your own body temperature with a forehead thermometer (bought from a chemist).
✧ Talk about the symbol 'nought' on the thermometer scale with the children. Explain it is sometimes called zero and means nothing or none. If we clench our fist when finger counting, this means nought.
✧ Fix a specially designed thermometer (from garden centres) onto the outside of your window to enable you to see how hot or cold it is outside from the inside of your room.
✧ Where would the red line on the thermometer reach on a very hot summer day? (About 30°C.)

SOUNDS LIKE A WINTER'S DAY

Objectives

Music – To develop sound awareness by listening to everyday noises.

Group size

The whole group.

What you need

A cardboard box approximately 50cm × 40cm to make a table screen (such as a shallow supermarket fruit tray), a variety of household objects to make their own sound or to represent other sounds such as an alarm clock, a pair of bedroom slippers, a toothbrush and comb, a pair of shoes with Velcro fastenings, a packet of cornflakes, spoon and bowl, a jug of water and a mug, a newspaper, an anorak with zip and a scarf, some rice and a flat cardboard box, a hairbrush, some pebbles in a plastic bottle.

What to do

Ask the children what kinds of sounds they might hear during a day. Ask them to be very quiet, to listen and watch while you use the items you have gathered. Make the sounds in the order in which they might be heard during the day. After you have made each sound, allow the children time to discuss when in the day they would hear it.

Start by setting off the alarm clock, then pad the slippers across a table top, brush the toothbrush across the comb (brushing teeth), fasten the Velcro on the shoes, pour cornflakes into the bowl and chink the spoon on the side, pour water into the mug, drop the newspaper onto a table top, zip up the anorak and wind the scarf around your neck and mouth to muffle your speech, pour the rice into the cardboard box to sound like rain, brush an opened newspaper to sound like the wind and tip the pebbles in their bottle to sound like feet crunching through snow.

Set the large box on its side to hide what you are doing. Repeat all the sounds in the same sequence and ask the children to tell you again when they would hear each one, for example when you make the sound with the Velcro, the children can say 'when I put my shoes on'.

Discussion

Which of these sounds are more likely to be heard in winter? (Muffled voices, rain, wind, feet crunching through snow.) What other winter sounds can you think of? (Ice cracking on puddles, gurgling from the central heating.)

Follow-up activities

✧ Let the children take it in turns to make the noises behind the screen for the others to guess.
✧ Make the sounds out of sequence and see if the children can still recognize them.
✧ Ask the children which of the sounds were quiet and which were loud.
✧ Encourage the children to make their own noises for winter sounds.

SNOWED IN

Objective

Geography — To make a curried rice dish using food grown in different countries.

Group size

Up to six children.

What you need

A heat source, a 2.5 litre saucepan and lid, a kettle, a measuring jug, a blunt pair of scissors for children and a sharp pair for an adult, a tin opener, a sieve, a teaspoon, a wooden spoon, a tablespoon, kitchen scales, a serving dish. Ingredients: a small onion, 50g of butter, 2 rounded teaspoons of curry powder, 4 cardamom pods, 225g of long grain rice, 0.6 litres of boiling water, 110g of frozen peas, a 420g tin of green lentils (from supermarkets), 110g of sultanas, 2 tablespoons of French dressing, salt and pepper.

What to do

Look at all the ingredients with the children and talk about whether they are dried, tinned, frozen or fresh and where they have originally been grown. Let the children share in the tasks of cutting, measuring and weighing to make this lentil rice dish.

Use the scissors to cut the onion into small pieces and then soften the pieces gently in the melted butter in the saucepan. Mix in the curry powder and the halved cardamom pods (cut with

scissors by an adult). Add the rice and the boiling water and simmer, covered, for about 25 minutes. The rice should be soft. Add the frozen peas and cook for a further five minutes. Drain the lentils and mix them into the rice — no further cooking is necessary. Finally, add the sultanas and moisten the rice mixture with the French dressing. Taste to see if salt and pepper are needed before tipping the lentil rice into the serving dish. Invite the children to taste the dish eating off play-house plates.

Discussion

Sometimes the winter weather is so wild that people may not be able to go to the shops to buy food. What kind of weather would prevent people from leaving their homes? (Violent storms or deep snow.) This is the time when people need to use food which they have stored. What kind of foods will store well? (Dried, frozen, tinned.) Food grown in other countries is often dried which means it can be sent on long journeys without going bad.

Follow-up activities

✧ Make a collection of foods which are likely to be stored in a food cupboard. Which of these has been grown in other countries?
✧ Sing the nursery rhyme 'Old Mother Hubbard'.
✧ Experiment with soaking dried foods — weigh them before and after soaking.
✧ Read the poem 'It's snowed' on page 69.

IT'S COLD OUTSIDE

Objectives

Art – To crayon white on a picture and practise cutting skills.

Group size

Six children.

What you need

A tin of baby talcum powder, a selection of toy people, bikes and cars (from construction sets), plastic building bricks, a tray, some fallen twigs, a rubber band and a glass jar to hold the twigs, six white crayons, six pairs of children's scissors, six copies of photocopiable page 92 copied onto blue sugar paper.

Explain to the children that when there is a light snowfall it looks just like everything has been covered with talcum powder. Note where the powder has landed on everything.

Give each child a copy of photocopiable page 92 and a white crayon. Talk about what is on the picture and ask the children to crayon anywhere that they think light snow would land. When they have finished ask them to cut the picture along the dotted lines to make their own jigsaw puzzle.

Discussion

When snow falls in winter it clings to the tops of everything. The twigs you have used are like a winter tree in the snow. Where did the snow land on them and what colour is the underneath part of the twigs? Which parts of the toys were covered in white? Have you noticed that anything which 'sticks out' will collect powder or snow on top?

Preparation

Copy the photocopiable sheet onto blue sugar paper. Secure the twigs together with the rubber band so that they look like a winter tree with bare branches.

What to do

Arrange the toy people, bikes and cars and plastic building blocks on the tray and let the children take it in turns to hold the talcum powder container above the tray and gently shake the powder over the top of the toys. Support the bunch of twigs in the jar and again sprinkle the powder onto the twigs from above.

Explain that if the snow was very deep on the ground everything would be buried. Doing jigsaw puzzles is a fun thing to do when you have to stay inside during winter time.

Follow-up activities

✧ Fit the jigsaw pieces together to see your snow picture again.
✧ Place a box, a ball and a toy car onto a sheet of dark coloured paper. Sprinkle powder or flour over them. Remove them carefully and see what shape is left on the paper.
✧ Look at commercially made jigsaw puzzles and talk about the corner pieces, the edge pieces and fitting the bumps into the dips!

KEEP STRETCHING

Objectives

PE – To do stretching exercises and find out that they can make you warm.

Group size

The whole group.

What you need

A non-slip area of flooring.

What to do

Show the children how people stand huddled up when they want to keep warm, with their arms wrapped tightly round themselves. Ask them to try this out. Tell the children that stretching your body out can also make you warm. Ask them to take off their shoes and socks and then to copy the following exercises.

• Stand up very straight with your feet a little apart and imagine that you are growing out of the ground. Make your arms and shoulders feel loose and stretch your neck and head up to the sky like a tree.

• Still keeping your body very straight, raise your arms above your head and try to touch the ceiling with your fingers.

• Bend your body in half at the waist and let your head and arms dangle towards the floor — like a floppy rag doll.

• Get on all fours like a dog then lift your bottom up in the air before straightening your legs, then straightening your arms and dropping your head down. You will look like a stretching dog.

• Kneel on all fours again and this time arch your back and say 'meow' then hollow your back and say 'puss'. This is how a cat stretches.

• Lie on your tummy and stretch your arms out. Then move your hands back to your shoulders and place them flat on the floor, lift up your head and trunk and hiss like a snake.

When the children have tried these exercises a few times and are nice and warm, tell them to lie on their backs as flat as pancakes and let their bodies relax and go floppy. Stay relaxed like this for a few minutes.

Discussion

Which action made you warmer — huddling up or stretching out? Sometimes during the winter you can feel cold even when you are inside the house. Running around would make you warm but there may not be enough room for this. You can always warm up by doing some of these 'still' exercises!

Follow-up activities

✧ Make a stretchy circle by all sitting on the floor in a circle with your legs wide apart. The children will need to shuffle backwards until their legs are stretched to their widest and yet they are still able to touch their neighbours with their feet. Can you touch each other with your outstretched hands?

✧ Show children how to sit cross-legged, back to back with a friend and gently rock backwards and forwards keeping their backs touching all the time.

WORD GAMES

Objective

English – To notice vowel sounds in the middle of words.

Group size

Four children.

What you need

A game of SCRABBLE◊, a large egg tray for sorting (30cm x 30cm).

Preparation

Sort the Scrabble letters into alphabetical order into the egg tray, putting duplicates on top of each other. The children may be able to help you.

What to do

Show the children the game of Scrabble and the sorted tiles, explain that they are all capital letters and say the sounds of the letters with them. Ask which egg carton compartment holds the most letters. (A E and I.)

Remove the five piles of vowels, build them into towers and explain that these are called the 'busy' letters because at least one of them is needed to make each word.

Encourage the children to help you make different words with the Scrabble tiles (use the word-families, listed here).

	Word families	
bad	lad	pad
den	hen	men
fin	pin	tin
cog	fog	jog
but	cut	hut

Sound out the letters of each word and ask the children to choose the appropriate tiles and place them on the Scrabble board. Place the words in each word-family underneath each other. Ask the children to point out the 'busy' letter in each word.

SCRABBLE◊ is a registered trademark of JW Spear & Sons PLC, Leicester LE3 2WT, England.

Discussion

During the winter months we are often stuck in the house for long periods of time. Why can't we go out and play? (Too wet or too cold.) We have to find indoor games to play. Have you seen your parents or older brothers and sisters playing Scrabble? What can you make with Scrabble letters? (Words.) Why are the letters A E I O U called the 'busy' letters? You may want to explain that 'y' is sometimes used as a vowel.

Follow-up activities

✧ Make a vertical word to cross one of the horizontal words on the board. This is called a crossword. (Explain the difference between 'cross' meaning anger and 'cross' meaning position!)
✧ Spell out your name using the tiles on the Scrabble board. Are any of the letters the same as your friend uses? How many vowels does your name have?
✧ Practise writing out the vowel sounds in capital and lower case letters.
✧ On squared paper, ask the children to write out all the alphabet letters – one in each square like on a Scrabble board.
✧ Share the poem 'Anyone bored?' on page 68.

SORT THE SUITS

Objectives

Mathematics – To sort and order playing cards.

Group size

Four children.

What you need

A pack of playing cards, a piece of A4 white card, a black and red marker pen.

Preparation

Remove the jokers and the 12 picture cards from the pack, they will not be needed for this activity. Shuffle the rest of the pack. In each quarter of the sheet of white card, draw one of the four playing card symbols – a red heart and diamond, a black spade and club. This is your symbol card.

What to do

Sit the children round a table and show them the number cards from the pack. Hold up several cards one at a time and establish that cards are either red or black. Ask the children what else they notice about the cards – each has a different number and symbol on it. Show them the symbol card that you have prepared and tell them the names of the suits – spades, hearts, diamonds, clubs.

Deal the cards into four piles and give one pile to each child. Place the symbol card in the middle of the table and ask the children to match their cards onto the central symbol card. It doesn't matter in what number order the cards are placed at this stage. When the cards have been sorted according to the symbol, give all the spades to one child, all the hearts to another and the diamonds and clubs likewise. Point out that the card with an 'A' on it is the ace and has only one 'pip' in the middle, this represents number one. Ask the children to sort their cards into number order starting with the ace.

Discussion

When cold winter weather makes it impossible to go out to play you have to find things to do inside the house. What sort of table games could you play inside? (Ludo, Snakes and ladders.) Playing cards can be used for all sorts of table games. What other games can you play inside which aren't table games? (Hunt the thimble, Hide-and-seek.)

Follow-up activities

✧ Use the picture cards from the pack and sort them into Kings, Queens and Jacks, or according to their symbol, or just into sets of reds and blacks.
✧ Look at the jokers from a pack of cards. Talk about how a jester used to be a member of the royal court to make the Royal Family laugh.
✧ How many Kings, Queens and Jacks are there in a pack of cards?
✧ Say the nursery rhyme 'The Queen of Hearts She Made Some Tarts'.

CHAPTER 4
ANIMALS IN WINTER

Animals adapt to cold winter weather in different ways, some fly away to warmer climates or hide away in dens for a long sleep, others grow thicker coats or change colour to blend with winter shades which will make them safer from predators. This chapter looks at aspects of animals' winter behaviour including their movement, food and how they can help man.

WINTER FODDER

Objectives

English – To be able to recognize written labels for animal foods and to match the labels accordingly, to the actual foods.

Group size

Five children.

What you need

A turnip, a swede, some green curly kale (from a greengrocer), hay (from a pet store), bran (from a health-food shop), five sheets of A4 card, a black marker pen.

Preparation

Write the words turnip, swede, kale, hay and bran separately onto each card.

What to do

Display the foods, name them and tell the children that animals eat these foods during winter. Let the children handle the foods and discuss what each type feels like. For example, hay is dry and prickly, turnips and swedes are smooth and heavy, kale is curly and leathery, bran is flaky and light.

Show the name cards of the foods and see if any of the children can read them. Help them to 'guess'

the words by sounding out the initial letter. Let the children take it in turns to place the name cards next to the appropriate food.

Discussion

During winter when grass and most plants stop growing, animals have to eat other foods. Many farm animals such as sheep, cows, pigs and horses eat food such as hay and root vegetables. This bulky food is known as fodder. Root vegetables are chopped up in a special machine before they are fed to the animals. Do you know what hay is made from? (Dried grass.) Some cut grass is kept moist in huge black plastic parcels, this grass turns into silage which is fed to cows during winter. Horses like to eat bran which is made from the outer parts of grain.

Follow-up activities

✧ Place a name card against the wrong food and see if the children can spot the error.
✧ Blindfold a child and let her/him smell each type of food and guess what it is.
✧ Read the story of 'The Enormous Turnip' in *Traditional Story Activities* by Jenny Morris (Scholastic).
✧ Talk about how hay is made and stored in bales. Make mini bales of hay securing them with rubber bands.
✧ Use construction toys to make a machine which could chop root vegetables.
✧ Cut the animal foods into pieces and use it to make facial features on a plate.

HOME BIRDS

Objectives

Art – To practise cutting and colouring skills and to make a 'running robin'.

Group size

Four children.

What you need

A piece of thick card 15cm × 10cm, two sheets of A4 white card, four circles of card with 8cm diameters, pencils, scissors, red and brown wax crayons, black felt-tipped pens, a skewer (for adults only) and lump of Plasticine, four split pins, a coloured picture of a robin.

Preparation

Draw the outline of a robin on the thick card and cut it out to make a template. Use this template to

make four separate robin cut-outs on the white card. Draw a feint pencil cross on each circle to divide it into quarters. Make a hole in the centre of each circle by pushing the skewer through the card and into the Plasticine.

What to do

Show the children the robin picture and explain that you want them to make their own running robin. Give each child a white robin cut-out and ask them to colour it on one side using the red and brown crayons in the appropriate places. See if they can show you with their finger where the eye should be and then let them draw an eye using the black felt-tipped pen. Make a hole in each child's robin's breast – 1cm in from the lower edge. Give a circle to each child and ask them to draw four identical robin legs and feet with the black felt-tipped pen. Use the feint pencil lines as a guide.

Place the robin over the circle of legs, line up the holes and attach them together using the split pin. Hold the robin's tail and push it along a flat surface to see it running! You may have to loosen the split pin slightly.

Discussion

Some birds find that winter is too cold for them so they fly away to warmer places. Most robins in this country stay in our gardens throughout the year even though it may be very cold. Why is a robin called robin redbreast? A robin has red feathers on its face and neck as well as on its breast. Robins become very brave during winter when they are short of food. They will perch very near gardeners who are digging the earth to see if they can catch any worms which have been turned over in the soil.

Follow-up activities

✧ Sing the nursery rhyme 'The North Wind Doth Blow' with the children.
✧ Dip some feathers into red paint and stick them onto your robin's breast.
✧ Tuck your head under your arm like birds tuck their heads under their wings to keep warm.
✧ Read the poem 'Robin rhyme' on page 70.

A WINTER HOLIDAY

N   S

Objective

Geography – To find out in which direction birds fly when they migrate for the winter.

Group size

The whole group.

What you need

A globe of the world or an atlas, a compass, a small piece of Plasticine and a little feather (from a feather duster!).

Preparation

Mould the Plasticine into a bird shape and push the feather into its back.

What to do

Tell the children that some birds fly south for the winter (see Discussion). Show them the compass and point out that the red end of the needle always points in the direction of north and the other end to the south. Let the children touch and move the globe of the world (or look in the atlas). Explain that this picture of the world shows where the land and the sea are. At the top of the globe is a place called the north pole which is very cold all the time. Show them where the British Isles are and position the Plasticine bird there. Move the 'bird' down the outside of the globe and tell the children that it is flying in a south direction to warmer weather. Point out the hottest area which is across the middle of the globe (the Equator). Let the children take it in turns to move the 'bird' from the British Isles to land in Africa in the south.

Discussion

Once winter sets in, the weather gets too cold for plants to grow and for insects to fly around. This means that there is a shortage of food for the birds

to eat. At this time of year some birds such as swallows and cuckoos, start to migrate or travel south to warmer places where food is more plentiful. Other animals such as reindeer and some whales also move to warmer areas for the winter.

There are some birds which stay here all year. Can you name any of them? (Robin, blackbird, thrush, doves, sparrow, the tit family.) When the weather gets warmer in Britain what happens to the birds who migrated for the winter? (They fly back here again.)

Follow-up activities

✧ Hold a compass and watch what happens to the needle when you turn round.
✧ At midday the sun shines from the south. Check this out with the compass.
✧ Write a large 'S' on a card and a large 'N' on another. Fix these cards to the walls at either end of you room. Ask the children to flap their arms like wings flying and to swoop to either the 'N' (North) or the 'S' (South).
✧ Read the poem 'Reindeer' on page 70.

MAKE A DEN

Objectives

Design and Technology — To plan and make a winter den in which to hibernate!

Group size

Four children.

What you need

A large piece of fabric such as an old sheet or some net curtains, cushions, car rugs or blankets, books, toys, games, a torch, a very large cardboard box such as from a washing machine (optional).

What to do

Explain to the children that some animals such as hedgehogs, ladybirds, frogs and snakes take a long rest during winter time (they hibernate). They eat lots of food until they feel really full up, then they go and find a quiet hidden place to be their den. They stay asleep in their den until the warmer weather comes.

Ask the children where they might make a den which would be very private. Suggest that it could be in a quiet corner behind some furniture or under a table, or even in a big cardboard box. Let them plan how they can make it more private (with a cover over it) and what they want to put in it, such as cushions, rugs or blankets, books, toys and games, a torch. Ask them to gather together all the things that they will need to make their den and then to spend some time resting and playing in it.

Discussion

Animals which hibernate through the winter don't play or eat. They spend their time asleep. Would you be able to go without food or play for the whole of winter? Hedgehogs hide under leaf piles, frogs bury themselves at the bottom of muddy ponds, snakes hide around tree roots and ladybirds hide in dried plant stems or under tree bark. Spiders like the warmth and come inside to hide for the winter. Where do you go when you want to have a rest or sleep? (Bed.)

Follow-up activities

✧ Paint leftover conker cases with thick brown paint to look like hedgehogs.
✧ Tear up newspaper into strips to make a den for toy animals to hide under.
✧ Cut small circles of red card and mark them with different numbers of black dots to make ladybirds. Arrange these ladybirds in order starting with the least number of dots and ending with the creature who has the most dots.
✧ Curl yourself up into a small ball and then uncurl as if you were a hedgehog waking up after a long winter's sleep.
✧ Read the poem 'Hibernating hedgehog' on page 73 and read the story 'The winter hedgehog' on page 74.

SAINT BERNARD

Objectives

RE – To hear the story about Saint Bernard and his dogs and find out how animals can help us during winter.

Group size

The whole group.

What you need

A picture of a Saint Bernard dog, see 'Dogs' *Collins Gems* (Harper Collins).

What to do

Tell the children the story of Saint Bernard. He was a monk who lived long ago in the mountains in Switzerland. He often walked in the mountains and knew his way around them very well. Sometimes people who were travelling in the mountains became so cold that they couldn't walk any further. Saint Bernard would take them back to his house and give them food and shelter for a while. Other people became lost or buried by the snow and if Saint Bernard couldn't find them, his big

rescue dogs could sniff out where the people were hidden. The dogs would also lick the cold people to keep them warm until more help came. These big dogs are now called Saint Bernard dogs after the famous monk.

When you have finished discussing the story, tell the children that you are going to play a game of hide-and-seek. Pick one child to be the Saint Bernard dog and ask him/her to wait outside your room while the other children hide. When everyone has hidden let the 'Saint Bernard' come into the room to find all the children. The last child to be found can now take a turn at being the dog.

Discussion

Saint Bernard and his dogs spent their time helping others in wintry conditions. Do you know of any other dogs who help out in the winter? Sheep dogs are specially trained by farmers to round up sheep when they need to be sheared or when they need to be fed with hay in winter. These dogs can also find sheep which have been buried under deep snow. Can you think of any other dogs which are particularly helpful to people? (Guide dogs for the blind and hearing dogs for the deaf.)

Follow-up activities

✧ Let the children look for Switzerland on a globe or a map of Europe.
✧ Find out more about Guide dogs for the blind by contacting RNIB (see Resources on page 96).
✧ If dogs can help us, can you think of ways in which we can help them? (Brushing, feeding, giving fresh water, taking for walks, petting them.)
✧ Carry out the assembly 'Asking for help' on page 66.

MOVE ALONG

Objectives

Drama — To mime the movement of animals during winter.

Group size

Six children.

What you need

A chair (to act as a bird table), pictures of cows, rabbits, sparrows, owls and ducks.

What to do

Explain to the children that cows graze in fields when the grass is growing during warm weather. During the winter, they just stand patiently huddled together waiting to be fed by the farmer. Ask the children to imagine that they are cows waiting to be fed — how will they move when the farmer loads some bales of hay into a rack? They will need to pull the hay through the bars with their mouths.

Birds can't get worms or insects from the earth when the ground is frozen hard or covered with snow. They sometimes stand on one leg keeping the other leg warm in their feathery body. Can you stand on one leg like a bird? Do birds have difficulty balancing? Put the chair in the middle of the room and pretend to put food on it. Ask the children to flock to the 'bird table'. Is there any pushing and quarrelling to get to the food?

Rabbits which can't nibble at snow-covered grass get so hungry that they have to gnaw the bark of young trees. Ask the children to mime this action and at the same time to use their hands like rabbits' ears, listening out for enemies while they are feeding.

Owls, who are night birds, will venture out in the day when there is snow on the ground — hoping to catch a mouse or little bird who is desperately looking for food. Ask the children to glide round like an owl looking for prey.

When ponds are frozen over, ducks can no longer swim. Ask the children to mime how ducks would slip and slide on the ice.

Discussion

Usually when we see farm animals and wild animals they are feeding or looking for food. Why are animals easier to watch during the winter? (Less greenery in which to hide.) During winter when food is in short supply, animals which are hungry may come very near to the house — they will take greater risks to find food. This is when you might be able to take a close look at a fox or a squirrel.

Follow-up activities

✧ Examine the animal pictures to see if you can tell from their size and shape whether they move quickly or slowly.
✧ Put some bird seed out on a bird table and see the different types of bird which come to feed.
✧ Talk about how some animals grow thick winter coats to cope with the cold.

PICK A NUT

Objective

Mathematics – To practise adding and subtracting while playing a board game.

Group size

Four children.

What you need

Photocopiable page 93, a sheet of A4 card, laminated paper (optional), a dice numbered 1–6 and a shaker pot, four differently coloured counters or bottle caps, approximately 40 acorns in a container (use buttons or counters if you haven't got acorns).

Preparation

Copy photocopiable page 93 onto the card and laminate it (optional).

What to do

Let the children each have a turn at throwing the dice and telling you which number they scored. In this way you can ensure that the children know their numbers one to six. The child with the highest number can be first to start the game.

Show the children the photocopiable sheet and ask them to tell you what is on it. Explain that the nuts on an oak tree are called acorns and that at the beginning of winter some acorns and a few dried leaves are still attached to the tree. (Oak trees are late in shedding their leaves.)

To play the game of 'Pick a nut', the first child should put his counter on the 'start' position on the board and collect three acorns immediately. He should now throw the dice and move along the board the number of squares shown. If he lands on an acorn he can pick one out of the container and add it to his collection. If he lands on a squirrel it means that the squirrel arrived before him and the child has to give back an acorn. Each child takes it in turn to move along the board. The winner is the one who has the most acorns by the time they reach the finish.

Discussion

Squirrels love to eat acorns and are very greedy to collect as many as they can and hide them. Why do they hide them? (To store them for later when winter food is scarce.) Where do squirrels hide acorns? (They dig them into the ground or hide them under stones.)

Follow-up activities

✧ Use clay or playdough to mould some little acorns for the game of 'Pick a nut'.
✧ Get the toys out of the cupboard very slowly like a tortoise. Now put them away very quickly like a squirrel with fast jerky movements.
✧ Plant a single acorn into damp soil in a pot. Keep it in the dark until you notice it sprouting. Remember to keep the soil damp.
✧ Use a pencil to make writing patterns just like a squirrel's wavy tail.

HARE COLOURINGS

Objective

Art – To paint the outline of a hare so that it will blend into different backgrounds

Group size

Six children.

What you need

A picture of a hare and a rabbit, a piece of thick card 21cm × 15cm, a pencil, a pair of sharp scissors (for adults only), three sheets of thin white A4 card, three pots of brown paint and six thick-bristled paintbrushes, newspaper, six lolly sticks, sticky tape, a black marker pen, some very large pieces of brown and white paper, Blu-Tack.

Preparation

Cut each piece of thin card in half. Draw and cut out the outline of a hare on the thick card. Use this template to draw six copies of the hare onto the thin card.

What to do

Show the children the picture of the hare and ask them which animal it looks like. Compare the pictures of the rabbit and the hare and see if the children notice that the hare is much bigger and has longer ears than the rabbit. A hare's back legs and feet are much bigger than its front ones. Explain to the children that some hares change their fur colour at different times of year. If they live in very cold areas they can change their brown fur to white.

Line the table with newspaper and give each child a hare outline to lay on it. Ask them to paint the hare brown all over one side. When it is absolutely dry, fix a lollipop stick to the brown side with sticky tape. Mark an eye on the brown and also the white side of the hare using the thick black pen. Use Blu-Tack to fix the brown and white paper alternately on a stretch of wall. Demonstrate how the children can walk past the wallpaper holding up the hare, turning it to white or brown to match the colour of background they are passing.

Discussion

Some animals which don't hibernate need to adapt to winter weather. Why do some hare's change from brown to white in snowy areas? (They look like snow so enemies can't see them easily.) Baby hares are called leverets and can hop about on their own when they are very young. Baby rabbits are called kittens and they stay next to their mothers for a long time.

Follow-up activities

✦ What are baby dogs, cats, goats, cows, horses and sheep called?
✦ Read Aesop's fable 'The Hare and the Tortoise' in *Aesop's Fables* retold by Jacqueline Morley (Macdonald).
✦ Practise leaping across the room as if you were a hare using your strong back legs.
✦ Hares have excellent hearing and eyesight. Practise crossing a pretend road where you also need to have excellent hearing and eyesight.

CHAPTER 5
PLANTS IN WINTER

Show the children what to look for outside during winter. Point out the trees looking after their buds and the bright berries for the birds to eat. Investigate creamy catkins swinging and swaying in the wind, evergreen leaves and cones which can be used to decorate our houses, and even some hardy vegetables growing for us to eat.

LAMBS' TAILS

Objectives

Mathematics – To match one catkin tail to each drawing of a lamb.

Group size

Six children.

What you need

Some catkin clusters from a hazel tree, if these are not available then have a picture of catkins from a book such as 'Trees' *Eye Witness Explorers* series (Dorling Kindersley) and have some long tassels from a length of upholstery braiding. A photograph of a lamb from a book such as *Big Book of Baby Animals* (Dorling Kindersley), a pencil, a pair of sharp scissors (for adults only) and a piece of card 14cm × 14cm, sheets of A4 coloured paper, adhesive and spreaders, white chalk.

Preparation

Draw a picture of a lamb on the piece of card and cut round the outline to make a template. Use this template to draw three lambs on one sheet of coloured paper. Prepare one sheet for each child. Cut individual tassels from the braid if you do not have hazel catkins.

What to do

Give the children one catkin cluster each and let them handle it gently or show them the picture of catkins in the book. Count how many catkins there are on each cluster and ask the children to separate them. Discuss in which way a catkin is similar to a lamb's tail. (Soft, long, woolly.) Ask the children to chalk inside the lambs' outlines to make them white and then to stick one catkin onto each lamb to make a tail. How many tails are there and how many lambs?

Discussion

Towards the end of the winter, before the leaves have started to grow on the hazel tree, you should be able to see creamy yellow catkins hanging from its bare branches. How many catkins did each cluster have? Did it vary? Catkins are a type of woolly flower and most of them hang down so that they can swing and sway in the wind. The soft furry flowers of pussy willow which ripen after the winter are also catkins but they don't hang and swing.

Follow-up activities

✧ Sing the nursery rhyme 'Little Bo-Peep Has Lost Her Sheep'.
✧ Blindfold one child at a time to see if they can pin a plaited woolly tail onto an enlarged picture of a lamb.
✧ Try placing a cluster of catkins to hang round each ear to look like dangling earrings!

GREEN NAMES

Objectives

English – To recognize which letters are used in our names and to rearrange them into the correct order.

Group size

Four children.

What you need

Four pieces of card (approximately 8cm × 20cm), a black marker pen, a container to store the leaves, a variety of evergreen leaves such as laurel, ivy, skimmia, non-prickly holly, camellia, rhododendron. You will need enough leaves to write all the letters used in each child's name, plus a spare one of each kind of leaf.

Preparation

Use the marker pen to write a name card for each child. Then write a letter on the back of each evergreen leaf to spell out the names of each of the children. Store the leaves mixed up in the container. Remember to use capitals for initial letters.

What to do

Lay out the spare unmarked leaves, shiny side up, and ask the children to pick up a leaf and feel the surface. Ask them to turn their leaf over, to look carefully and then to feel the surface of this side also. They can repeat this procedure with each variety of leaf. Remove these leaves and introduce the marked ones.

Lay them out on the table, shiny side up, and when the children turn them over, see if they can recognize the letters. Give the children their name cards and ask them to select the leaves which have the letters of their name. Ask them to arrange the letters in the same order as they are written on their name card. Ensure the children wash their hands after handling the leaves.

Discussion

Some trees and bushes which have very soft thin leaves drop them for the winter. How would you describe the leaves you have just handled? (Tough, thick, glistening and shiny.) Did you notice the veins on the underside? Why do you think these leaves are called evergreens? (Because they stay on the trees or bushes and are green throughout the year.) Their waxy thickness protects them from being damaged by the winter cold. People decorate their homes with evergreen leaves during the winter because they are so bright and colourful. Many evergreen bushes produce winter berries for the birds to eat.

Follow-up activities

✧ Push some evergreen leaves through a piece of card and tape the stems securely at the back. Hang up the card to make a winter decoration.
✧ Press the veiny underside of an evergreen leaf into some rolled out playdough to make leaf impressions.
✧ Sort and match a variety of evergreen leaves into their different types.
✧ Read the poem 'A puzzle – What am I?' on page 71 to the children.

CONE TREES

Objectives

Design and Technology — To select a base for a painted fir cone and make a bright, attractive decoration for winter.

Group size

Six children

What you need

A branch with needle-like leaves from a conifer tree, a mixture of pine cones for examining and decorating, a selection of bottle caps large enough for the cones to sit in, some Plasticine or Blu-Tack, ready-mixed powder paints in several different colours, paintbrushes of different thickness, PVC adhesive, glitter.

Preparation

Add a little adhesive to each paint pot and mix it in thoroughly.

What to do

Let the children handle the conifer branch and the selection of cones. Point out that some cones have open scales and some are tightly shut. Show them how a cone shape tapers from a round fat part to a point.

Explain that you want them to make little cone trees and let them choose a cone and a suitable bottle cap in which the cone can sit. Ask the children to fix their cone into the cap with a lump of Plasticine. If they have chosen a cone with open scales encourage them to choose an appropriately sized paintbrush which will go in between the scales.

After they have painted their trees they can quickly sprinkle some glitter on before the paint dries, to make sparkly winter decorations.

Discussion

Most conifer trees are green during the winter. Their branches have needle-shaped leaves which are thin and spiky, and are tough enough to last throughout the cold weather.

Pine cones or fir cones grow on these trees and sometimes take two years before they are ripe and ready to fall off. Which cones in the collection are the younger ones? (Those with hard, tightly shut scales.) The older cones have larger scales which open on warm dry days so that their ripe seeds can scatter. Can you describe what the cones feel like? (Rough, bumpy, knobbly.) What else is cone shaped? (Ice-cream wafers, road cones.)

Follow-up activities

✧ Choose two ripe fir cones of similar size. Leave one near a radiator overnight. Compare the cones next day and see if the warmer one has opened up.

✧ Press some tin foil gently over a ripe pine cone — does the foil look like a 'pine'apple?

✧ Curl up like a tight little young fir cone — gradually open up like a big ripe fir cone.

✧ Make some paper road cones to use with the toy cars. Colour circles of paper in orange. Make a cut into the centre and wrap the circle round until it overlaps into a cone. Secure it with sticky tape. Do the cones stack easily?

TWIGGY

Objective

Science – To find out if living bare twigs will show their hidden leaves, under the right conditions towards the end of winter.

Group size

The whole group.

What you need

A variety of winter twigs freshly pruned from bare trees and shrubs such as beech, weeping willow, pussy willow, horse-chestnut, oak, apple, pear, hazel, honeysuckle, flowering blackcurrant. A clear glass vase or jar, some water in a jug, a magnifying glass, a chopping board, a pair of secateurs and sharp craft knife (for adults only).

What to do

Hand out the twigs for the children to examine and remind them to be careful of their own and other people's eyes. Ask them to run their fingers gently up the twig starting from the cut end and to look very carefully all the way along as they do this. Remove a big bud from a horse-chestnut twig and cut the bud along its length. Let the children look through a magnifying glass to examine what is inside the bud.

Place all the twigs in the vase and pour in water until it is half full. Leave the vase in the light and warmth where the children can see it every day. After about three weeks some of the buds should have opened up into leaves. Change the water in the vase frequently.

Discussion

When you ran your fingers along the twigs did you notice the bumps? These are the buds which will grow into leaves, flowers and new twigs. What did you see inside the horse chestnut bud? The woolly white bits are the beginnings of a new leaf which is tucked safely away during the cold weather of winter. Why do some of the leaves start to burst out of their buds once the twigs are inside the house? When the twigs come out of the cold they think that spring has arrived! All plants need water to grow.

Follow-up activities

✧ Look at the twigs to see whether the buds come opposite each other in pairs, or do they grow on the twig in steps. Draw some twigs and pencil the buds along them in pairs or steps.
✧ Lay the twigs out and arrange them in a line in order of length.
✧ Make a twiggy tree. Cut slits in the top of a cardboard tube and wedge in some fallen twigs collected from the garden.
✧ Describe the shapes of different winter trees and shrubs – tall, thin, short, round, spiky, curly.
✧ Which twig is the most friendly? When horse-chestnut leaves fall off their branch they leave a large scar which looks like a big smiling mouth!

FROZEN VEG

Objectives

Science – To find out which vegetables can survive the frosts of winter.

Group size

The whole group.

What you need

Some or all of the following vegetables: lettuce leaves, two chunks of cucumber, two tomatoes, two sprouts, two sticks of celery, two leeks, two leaves of winter cabbage or sprouting broccoli, two parsnips, two trays, a sharp knife (for adults only) and chopping board, use of a freezer.

Preparation

If a freezer is not available on your premises, freeze one of each kind of vegetable at home overnight. Next day, wrap these frozen vegetables in thick newspaper and take them in to your group. If you are bringing the frozen vegetables from home, do the activity first thing in the morning before the vegetables defrost!

What to do

Look together at the unfrozen vegetables and ask the children to handle them and then to name them. Discuss the textures, note the colours and feel whether the vegetables are hard or soft. Explain that you are going to put one of each kind of vegetable on a tray and into the freezer overnight as if they were outside during frozen winter weather. Keep the unfrozen vegetables cool on the other tray overnight.

Next day, let the children handle the frozen vegetables before leaving them to defrost at room temperature. Ask the children to report back to you any changes they see as the vegetables defrost. When the frozen vegetables are completely defrosted, compare them to the tray of unfrozen vegetables.

Discussion

In which way had the vegetables from the freezer changed overnight? (They had frozen hard.) What did each vegetable look and feel like when it had thawed out? (Wet, rubbery, slimy, burst open, darkened.) Which of the vegetables survived the extreme cold the best? Salad vegetables are watery and have thin leaves which cannot live outside during the winter. Leeks, winter cabbage, sprouts, parsnips and sprouting broccoli are all hardy vegetables and can live outside in wintry conditions.

Follow-up activities

◇ Sow lettuce seeds in two pots and keep one inside and one outside. Which seeds germinate?
◇ Chop up some fresh salad vegetables, add some yoghurt dressing and enjoy a mixed salad.
◇ Give each child a sprout to peel completely and make a high pile of leaves.
◇ Use scissors to make several cuts lengthwise down towards the base of a thin leek. Leave it to soak in cold water overnight and next day see how it has curled.
◇ Cut some holes in a thick winter cabbage leaf. Stick your fingers through it and 'walk' it to pretend you are a cabbage creature!

WINTER FARE

Objective

Art – To make a collage, using dried material such as seed heads, grasses and fallen leaves.

Group size

Four children.

What you need

Four plain white paper plates (approximately 20cm diameter), a collection of different leaves which have fallen on the ground, flowers, seed heads and grasses, two pots of adhesive and spreaders, a stapler, four pencils, four pairs of scissors, four pencils, a pair of secateurs (for adults only).

Preparation

Collect dried winter material from a garden, such as dried heads from hydrangeas, Michaelmas daisies, poppies and thistles, cow parsley and red campion, together with all grasses including ornamental ones. Ferns and beech leaves can also be used. The children may be able to help in collecting material themselves.

What to do

Give a paper plate to each child and ask them to write their names on the back. Ask them to cut some short pieces of dried material and arrange them around the plate with the stems lying on the outside rim. If necessary, help them with their arrangement by putting the heavier denser material at the bottom and the finer pieces on the top. When the children are happy with their arrangement help them to staple the stems round the rim of the plate. The beech leaves can be tucked behind the fixed stems or they can be stuck onto the plate first.

Discussion

Some plants cannot live in the cold weather. Many keep their roots alive under the ground, but their flowers, leaves and stems wither, then lose their green colour and turn yellow or brown. Sometimes during winter, fallen leaves lose their fleshy part and have only their veins left – they look like skeletons! Often flowers dry out and leave a brittle head which allows seeds to escape and scatter. What kind of sound do dried leaves and flowers make? (Rustle, snap and crackle.) Little creatures often spend the winter hiding in dried plants – did you find any?

Follow-up activities

✧ Attach string to the plates and hang them up.
✧ Fill a pepper pot with dry sand and sprinkle it to show how seeds scatter from dried flower heads.
✧ If you find any seeds in the flower heads, plant them in a pot, cover them with plastic film and keep the pot warm and damp indoors. See what happens!
✧ Bend a piece of the dry collage material to see if it will curve like a piece of living plant?
✧ Look through a magnifying glass at any insects found among the plant material. Identify them using a book of insects such as 'Insects' *Eyewitness Explorers* series (Dorling Kindersley).
✧ Enjoy the poem 'Winter seeds' on page 72 together.

DOTTED FERNS

Objectives

English – To become familiar with the dot on the lower case letter 'i'.

Group size

The whole group.

What you need

If you do this activity early in the winter you will be able to find real fern fronds (leaves), if not use pictures from a gardening book such as *Gardeners' Encyclopaedia* (Royal Horticultural Society). A story book with large print, an A4 piece of card to make a fern template, sheets of green A4-sized paper, a pair of sharp scissors (for adults only), brown wax crayons.

Preparation

Draw a fern frond on the cardboard and cut it out to make a template. Use this template to make a paper fern frond on the green paper for each child. Cut out several fronds together.

What to do

Show the children the writing in the story book and point out the dots over the letter 'i'. With your finger make a vertical line in the air and then 'give it a dot'. Explain that this is how you write the letter 'i' and ask the children to copy your writing in the air. Encourage them to join in with the chorus 'give it a dot'!

Allow the children to handle the ferns, to smell them and to examine the underside of the fronds. Give them each a paper fern cut-out and ask them to dot it all over on one side. Ensure the children wash their hands after handling the fronds.

Discussion

Most ferns which grow outside are very tough and can survive well into the winter even after the first frosts. Ferns don't have flowers and therefore don't have seeds. Instead of seeds they have spore cases. These look like little orange-brown dots running along the back of their fronds. When the

spore case is ripe it bursts open and tiny little spores float into the air. Spores can grow into new fern plants. What do spore cases look like? (Dots on the letter 'i'.) Just before fern fronds open up they can be seen in a coil.

Follow-up activities

✧ Look for the letter 'i' in your own story books and also look for 'j's and full stops.
✧ Look at the way the dots are grouped on a dice and draw the same patterns on some paper.
✧ Play a game of dominoes by matching the dots.
✧ Prepare a page of large dots and ask the children to join some up to make different shapes.
✧ Randomly number some dots 1 to 10 and let the children join then in numerical order.
✧ Draw spirals to look like coiled fern fronds.

SIGNS OF SPRING

Objectives

Art – To cut paper leaves and make a snowdrop picture.

Group size

Six children.

What you need

A real snowdrop (available in February) or a picture from a gardening book such as *Gardeners' Encyclopaedia* (Royal Horticultural Society), two three-cornered white polystyrene packing chips for each child, sheets of dark green gummed-paper, six pairs of scissors, two pots of PVA adhesive and spreaders, six pieces of coloured card (21cm × 15cm).

Preparation

Cut 12 very narrow pieces of green, gummed paper about 12cm × 0.5cm. Stick two of these stems onto each coloured card.

What to do

Look at the snowdrop flower with the children and count its long outer petals and its inner petals. Compare the shape of the triangular polystyrene chips to the snowdrop shape. Show the children how to run their fingers along the stem and leaves noticing the long narrow shapes.

Let them cut long strips out of the gummed paper to make similar shaped leaves. Position the leaves vertically in pairs either side of each stem on the card and then stick them into place. Ask the children to count out two polystyrene chips each and stick them to the tops of the stems to complete the picture of snowdrops.

Discussion

Some flowers can live in cold weather. When snowdrops appear we know that its getting towards the end of winter. Snowdrops are one of the first signs of spring. When they start to grow, their buds point straight up to the sky but eventually they bend over so that the flowers face the ground. How many long outer leaves does a snowdrop have? What is a three-cornered shape called? Where else do we see triangular shapes? (Road signs, percussion triangle.) Have you noticed any other flowers which appear in winter such as yellow winter jasmine and winter aconites?

Follow-up activities

✧ Arrange the snowdrop pictures side by side along the bottom of your window to look as if they are growing outside.
✧ Snowdrops look like little drops of snow. What other drops can you think of? (Teardrops, chocolate drops, raindrops, dew drops.)
✧ Examine a snowdrop after its white flower has disappeared. Cut open the hard green pod and see where all the seeds are forming.
✧ Fold a square of paper in half diagonally and cut it along the fold to make two triangles. Fold each triangle into half to make more triangles and cut again. Fit the triangles back into a square again. (Tip: arrange all the 'short' points to meet in the middle.)
✧ Read the poem 'My treasure' on page 73.

CHAPTER 6
WINTER CELEBRATIONS

The chance to celebrate helps brighten up the dark days of winter. On Burns' Night and New Year's Eve people hold parties, at Hanukkah and the winter solstice we light candles and fires, and at Christmas and Valentine's Day we give cards.
In this chapter, there are activities to celebrate all
these occasions

HALF-HEARTED

Objectives

Mathematics – To prick out half a heart and make a symmetrical pattern.

Group size

Six children.

What you need

Six pieces of thin white paper (12cm × 16cm), six pieces of A4 red card, six sharp pointed pencils, two sticks of adhesive, some glitter, six carpet tiles (not necessary if you have a carpeted area in your room).

Preparation

Fold each piece of white paper down the middle (along the side measuring 12cm), and draw half a heart outline up to the fold. Fold the pieces of red card in half to make a steep roof top shape.

What to do

Talk to the children about St Valentine's Day (see Discussion). Tell them you would like them to make their own Valentine card.

Hand out the pieces of folded white paper and ask the children to place it either on a carpet tile or on the carpeted floor. Show them how to push the pencil point firmly through the double paper to make holes all along the edge of the half heart outline. When they have finished ask them to open up the paper and see what shape they have made. Stick the opened heart shape onto the outside of the red card and dab the adhesive stick randomly across it. Sprinkle some glitter over these sticky dabs to decorate the heart.

Discussion

Saint Valentine's Day is on 14 February each year which is near the end of winter. This is the day when people send a card to the person whom they love. Often they do not even put their name on the card but leave it blank for the person to guess who sent it. Usually, the card has a picture of a heart on it. If you send your Valentine card to a boyfriend or girlfriend he/she is called your 'sweetheart'. Who will you give your card to – Mum or Dad or a grandparent? Some Valentine cards have a picture of two little birds standing very close together – they are called lovebirds!

Follow-up activities

✧ Put your hand on your heart and see if you can feel it bumping!
✧ Prick out some other symmetrical shapes such as a circle, a rectangle, a triangle and an oval.
✧ Make a heart display – see page 63.

FLAT AS A PANCAKE

Objective

History – To learn about the traditions of Shrove Tuesday.

Group size

The whole group to see the pancake made and four children at a time for the game.

What you need

For the pancakes: 100g plain flour, 250ml milk, one egg, pinch of salt, 50g butter, frying pan, metal spatula, mixing bowl and whisk, plate, heat source. A large and small paper plate for each child, ready-mixed yellow and brown paint and paintbrushes.

Preparation

Make up the pancake batter by whisking all the ingredients (with the exception of the butter) together in the bowl.

What to do

Explain to the children that on the Tuesday before the festival of Lent (Shrove Tuesday), people celebrate by making pancakes from eggs, milk and flour. Show them how to make the pancake. Heat a little butter in the frying pan to grease the whole surface. Pour in some of the batter mix, to cover the base of the pan when tilted. Using the spatula, loosen the pancake and then hold the pan handle with both hands and flick the pancake over. When it is cooked, turn it onto a plate for the children to see. Sometimes pancakes fall on the floor when they are being tossed – which the children love!

Tell the children that you want them to paint a pancake on a paper plate. Give them each a small paper plate for them to paint all over on both sides with the yellow and brown paint. When the paint is dry, give each child a large paper plate on which to rest their 'pancake'. Show them how to try and flick their 'pancakes' up into the air so that they turn over and can be caught on the bigger plate. Tell them this is called 'tossing the pancake'.

Discussion

During Lent some people only have very simple food such as bread and water. This is to remind them of anything they may have done wrong. They use up other food items before Lent begins and making pancakes is a good way to use up eggs, flour and milk. People sometimes hold pancake races on Shrove Tuesday.

Follow-up activities

✧ Make some more pancakes with the batter and sprinkle orange juice and sugar on them before folding them ready to eat.
✧ See how many times you can catch the paper 'pancake'. How many times did your friend do it?
✧ Say the rhyme 'Mix a pancake' from *This Little Puffin...* compiled by Elizabeth Matterson (Puffin).
✧ Pancakes are very flat. Which other foods are also flat?

CANDLELIGHT

Objective

Design and Technology – To make a candle holder.

Group size

Four children.

What you need

A picture of or a real menorah (a branched candelabra), a candleholder, a collection of different types of candles including tree candles (which will fit into the menorah), catering candles, night lights and decorative candles (they can be part used), a tub of non-fire clay, a tray and a large damp cloth, clay tools and a hair comb (optional).

Preparation

Form eight pieces of clay into various sizes from the size of a plum to a grapefruit. Keep these clay pieces moist on the tray under a damp cloth.

What to do

Show the children the menorah and then the candleholder. Ask them to count how many candles both hold. Let them handle the candles you have collected and talk about their uses and their different attributes – thick or thin, long or short. Show them the wick and explain its use.

Tell the children you would like them to make a candleholder for one or more candles. Ask them to choose a candle(s) and a suitably sized piece of clay which can hold the chosen candle or candles. Let them work the clay to shape a candleholder and then push the candle(s) into it. If it topples over they will have to rework the shape or add more clay until the candleholder is stable. The

children can decorate the clay using the comb or tools and then leave it to dry in the air. Stress to the children that they must never light the candles on their own or they could get very badly hurt.

Discussion

Jewish people celebrate the festival of Hanukkah, usually in December, by lighting one candle each day for eight days. They remember the time when there was only enough oil left in the synagogue (place of worship) for one day and yet by a miracle it lasted for eight days. At Hanukkah, a special menorah is used which has eight branches and an extra candle at the front with which to light the other candles. A seven-branched menorah is usually used as a Jewish symbol. What are candles used for? (Source of light and for celebrations.)

Follow-up activities

✧ Pretend it is Hanukkah and light the candles in the menorah. Light one candle on the first day, two candles on the second, three on the third and so on until all eight candles are lit.
✧ Hebrew is a language written and spoken by some Jewish people. Look at the Hebrew alphabet and compare it to our alphabet.
✧ Sing 'Candles on the cake' from *This Little Puffin...* compiled by Elizabeth Matterson (Puffin).
✧ Sing the song 'Candlelight' on page 85.

CHRISTMAS NOTES

Objectives

Music – To introduce musical notation and to make a Christmas card.

Group size

Four children.

What you need

A book of music, such as a nursery rhyme book, thick card 6cm × 6cm, four pieces of A4 red card, pieces of silver card, white sequin strip, PVA adhesive, pots and spreaders, scissors, ruler, pencils.

Preparation

Draw a musical crotchet note on the thick card, cut it out and use this template to make the silver card notes. Cut carefully so that the silver side of the card leaves the crotchet facing the correct way. Cut out three silver notes for each child. Cut the sequin strip into lengths measuring 15cm × 3cm. Cut and discard a 5cm strip off the widest edge of each piece of red card.

What to do

Show the children the book of music and point out the written musical notes. Explain that the black and white dots with sticks are called notes. They are used to write down music in the same way that letters are used to write down words.

Give each child a piece of red card and help them to fold it in half to make a greetings card shape. Ask them to take a piece of sequin strip and stick

it down across the middle of the card and then to arrange and stick three silver notes on top. Help them to write inside their card to wish a 'Happy Christmas' to the person to whom they will give the card, and to write their own name to say who the card is from.

Discussion

A long time ago, people just remembered music in their heads. One day some monks invented a way of writing it down in the form of notes so that their music wouldn't be forgotten. They placed the notes on the lines or in the spaces of five lines – which look like a very wide ladder (called the stave). The white notes last for a longer time than the black notes.

What other ways do we have today for saving music? (Cassette tapes, CDs and video tapes.) People give Christmas cards as a symbol of peace and kindness.

Follow-up activities

✧ Give each child a copy of photocopiable page 94. Encourage them to ring the note which is different and then ask them to make all the notes in the row look the same.
✧ Let the children draw some notes in different positions on a blank stave. Notes drawn at the top will have sticks pointing downwards, and those at the bottom will have sticks pointing up.
✧ Experiment by blowing through a recorder and hearing different note sounds according to which holes are covered.
✧ Read the poem 'I've made a star' on page 73.

MONEY BOX

• •

Objectives

RE – To encourage charity and to make a money box.

Group size

Two children.

What you need

An empty cardboard box such as a biscuit packet (for cutting up), a copy of the box template on photocopiable page 95, two pieces of A4 thin card, a pair of sharp scissors and a craft knife (for adults only), crayons or felt-tipped pens, two 1p coins, a pot of PVA adhesive and spreaders or an adhesive stick, adhesive tape (optional).

Preparation

Copy the box template onto the thin card and cut round each template. Cut out the shaded section to make a slot.

What to do

Show the children the empty box and cut it open with the craft knife (keep out of reach of the children). Try to keep the box in one piece and then lay it flat. Ask the children to identify the flat shapes which made up the box.

Give each child a prepared template and compare it to the flattened box.

Explain that you want them to make a money box and ask them to colour the squares and tabs first. Help them to fold and crease along all the inside lines of the template and then spread some adhesive on each tab. Fold the template into a box shape, matching up the patterns on the tab with the patterns on the squares. Stick the tabs to the outsides of the box. Let the children push a 1p coin through the slot in each money box. Reinforce the

money box by sticking adhesive tape along the edges (optional).

Discussion

In the past, the priests opened the poor (collection) boxes in their churches on Boxing Day (the day after Christmas Day) and gave away the collected money. In later years rich people gave money in boxes to people who had helped them all year, such as their servants or the lamplighter. Nowadays, if we give money at Christmas to the people who help us, we don't bother to use a box. What do you give at Christmas to the people who help you?

Follow-up activities

✧ Encourage the children to take their box home and save money for people in need; stress that they need only save pennies.

✧ Invite someone from a charity (such as the Royal National Institute for the Blind or the Royal National Institute for Deaf People) to show a collection box and talk about the charity.

✧ Make a collection of money boxes including a piggybank.

✧ Look at some old money and compare it with the money we use now.

STRANGERS FIRST

Objectives

Music – To sing to some traditional music and make the appropriate actions.

Group size

The whole group.

What you need

A piece of coal, a piece of bread, the version of 'Auld Lang Syne' on page 87.

What to do

Talk to the children about New Year celebrations – see Discussion. In Scotland they have a party called Hogmanay and it has some special customs. The first person after midnight who sets foot in the house is supposed to bring luck for the whole year. He should be a dark-haired stranger and bring coal and bread as presents (let the children handle the coal and bread). This is supposed to mean that the people in the house will be warm and have enough food for the whole of the next year. Often somebody from the party pretends to be the stranger! When he has been let into the house, everyone forms a circle and sings the song 'Auld Lang Syne' which means 'for the sake of old times. Give the children time to practise singing the words to the tune of 'Auld Lang Syne'. Show them how to form a circle, crossing arms and holding hands. As you sing the song, all move round in the circle. When you sing the chorus, all move forwards towards the centre of the circle and then raise hands, but don't let go! Keep going in and out to the centre of the circle while singing the chorus!

Discussion

The end of our year is the last day in December which is in the middle of winter. On this evening, which is called New Year's Eve, people celebrate and have parties because they are happy that a New Year is about to begin. Some towns ring church bells at midnight. Australia is a country on the opposite side of the globe to the British Isles. While we have winter, Australia has summer and so the people there can celebrate the New Year by having barbecues on the beach in the hot sun.

Follow-up activities

✧ Find Australia and Scotland on a map.
✧ Draw some writing patterns in crosses like the children's arms were crossed during the song.
✧ Read the story of Cinderella and see what happened to her at midnight.
✧ Sing 'A happy new year to you' on page 84.

THE PLOUGHMAN POET

● ●

Objectives

RE – To grow a seed and witness the miracle of life.

Group size

The whole group.

What you need

50g of mixed seeds containing barley (obtainable from a pet shop as bird seed – barley from supermarkets won't grow), a glass bowl and jug of water, a paper towel, a shallow dish, some plastic film, a piece of newspaper.

Preparation

Separate some barley corn from the mixed seed then soak the barley in water overnight (to hasten germination). Note that in this activity the terms corn, grain and seed all have the same meaning.

What to do

Tell the children about Robert Burns whose birthday is celebrated on January 25th (1759). He was a Scottish farmworker who loved the countryside and wrote beautiful poetry. He wrote a poem called John Barleycorn – describing what happens to corn throughout the year. In winter, it is stored as a hard seed and in early spring, it is planted in the ground where it starts to sprout. During the summer, it grows into a tall grass and by autumn it is time to cut (harvest) it and separate the grain from the stalks.

Let the children feel the dry bird seed and point out which is the barley. Fold the paper towel and place it in the dish. Ask a child to thoroughly wet the towel with water and ask another to scatter the soaked barley corn onto it. Cover these grains with plastic film and then newspaper. Leave the dish in a warm place where the children can monitor what happens over the next week. Ask them to predict what will happen to the barley corn in the dish. Remove the newspaper when sprouting occurs – after about 36 hours.

Discussion

What happened to the barley corn in the dish? Grains in winter don't look very exciting but each seed holds a tiny bit of life which can grow into a green grass plant. Barley grain is used in soups and stews and to make barley-water drinks. Other corn grains can be crushed to provide flour and breakfast cereals. Some people (especially Scottish) have a party on Burns' Night. They serve haggis (a big round sausage) with mashed potatoes and 'neeps' (turnips).

Follow-up activities

✧ Make a collection of breakfast cereals. Which cereals are made from the grains of oats, maize (cornflakes), wheat and rice?

✧ Mix cornflour with water and let the children handle it to find out how strangely it behaves!

✧ Make some flapjack biscuits: melt 250g of margarine with four tablespoons of syrup, add 350g of porridge oats and 125g of demerara sugar. Bake in a flat tray in a medium oven for about 25 minutes until golden brown. Cool slightly then cut into squares.

THE SHORTEST DAY

Objectives

History – To discover how people in the past celebrated the middle of winter and to make a collage.

Group size

Six children.

What you need

Six large pieces of orange coloured sugar paper (approximately 30cm × 40cm), a pencil, three pots of PVA adhesive and six spreaders, a selection of dried and waste material such as leaves, newspaper, computer paper, corrugated cardboard, straw, grass.

Preparation

Draw a large triangle faintly in pencil on each piece of paper. Cut the corrugated cardboard into narrow strips to represent small twigs.

What to do

Explain to the children that some people celebrate the shortest day in the year, which is called the winter solstice, and falls on or about 21 December each year. Of course, all days are really as long as each other but winter days, which have less sunlight than summer days, seem to be shorter. In past times food could not be sent from hot countries like it is now and this meant that if there was not enough sunlight, crops could not ripen and people would be short of food. This is why people celebrated the shortest day because they knew that the days which followed would have more sunshine and would be 'longer'!

They built and burnt bonfires to honour the sun and welcome the longer days to come. Give each child a piece of sugar paper, some adhesive and a spreader. Ask them to name all the materials you have gathered and then to make a bonfire picture. They can tear or cut the materials and stick them randomly onto the paper, roughly within the triangle shape. Encourage the children to overlap the materials to give a three-dimensional effect like an unlit bonfire.

Discussion

A bonfire is a large outdoor fire. People put their garden waste into a big pile ready to burn as a bonfire. When the fire burns low, some people cook potatoes in the embers. Why should children stand well away from bonfires? (To avoid getting burned from flying sparks.)

Some people celebrate the winter solstice by keeping a log burning for days. They call it a Yule log and keep the ash for good luck.

Follow-up activities

✧ Cook some jacket potatoes in the oven like people do in bonfires.
✧ Use orange, yellow and brown crayons to 'scribble' a bonfire on a piece of white paper. Brush some thin black paint over the whole piece of paper to make it look like a burning bonfire at night.
✧ Sing the song 'I Love the Sun' from *Someone's Singing Lord* (A & C Black).

CHAPTER 7
WINTER DISPLAYS

Many of the winter activities that the children have completed can be used to provide interesting displays. Let the children share the task of displaying their work because although this may result in a less beautiful display, it is an excellent way of letting children know how much you value what they do.

WARM INDOORS

What you need

Pale blue frieze paper, four clear A4 plastic wallets, ready-mixed white powder paint and paintbrush, stiff white card cut into 6cm wide strips, corrugated cardboard or brown wrapping paper, dried grass or hay (from a pet shop), dried flower heads or any plants growing naturally in a winter garden, two sheets of white A4 paper, black and pale yellow wool, a pencil, PVA adhesive and spreaders, sticky tape, stapler, scissors, labelling card and a black marker pen.

What to do

Line a metre square display area with the frieze paper. Use a pencil to mark out the window frame area on the frieze paper (approximately 45cm × 65cm), then working within this frame, paint a few white clouds across the top area. Cut the corrugated card to represent a tree trunk and bare branches. Arrange this and the dried material inside the rest of the frame to look like a winter scene viewed through a window.

Staple the four plastic wallets over the winter scene, separating and surrounding the 'panes' with the white card to make a window frame. You made need to lift the 'panes' slightly with a cardboard spacer to accommodate the dry materials sticking out. Draw and cut the outlines of the back of the head and shoulders of two children. Colour the outlines and stick on wool for hair. Position these outlines as if they are looking out of the window. Label your display 'It's warmer inside'.

Vary the display by:
✧ drawing raindrops with a black dry-marker pen onto the plastic windows. Rub them off on dry days!
✧ painting white paint on the plastic windows as if snow is resting on the tops of the tree branches. Rub the paint away when the snow has melted!
✧ rubbing white chalk across the plastic windows as if they are steamed up with the warmth inside – like a bathroom when the hot water is running.

Discussion

What will the children be saying to each other as they look out of the window? Talk about having to stay indoors on bad winter days. Discuss the sort of things you could do while you have to stay inside (see 'Word games' on page 33 and 'Sort the suits' on page 34).

It's warmer inside.

WINTER WOOLLIES

●●●●●●●●●●●●●●●●●●●●●●●●●●●●●

What you need

Frieze paper or an old woollen blanket to line the display area. A large piece of thick paper, pencil and scissors. Grey felt and an old knitted garment which can be cut up (preferably in white, cream or black). Circles of card approximately 7cm in diameter, remnants of different coloured, thick knitting wool. Woollen items – a piece of carpet, a baby's blanket, socks, a scarf, a pom-pom hat, a cardigan, slippers and gloves. Card for labelling, a black marker pen, a stapler, a hole punch and some hook pins (from an educational supplier).

What to do

Draw a large outline of a sheep onto the thick paper, cut it out and cover its body with the old knitted garment – either in one piece or with unravelled wool. Staple the sheep's body into the middle of the lined display area. Cut its feet and face from the grey felt and draw in the face features. Attach the face and feet onto the sheep.

Make single coloured pom-poms by wrapping wool through double circles of card (see diagram). Hang the pom-poms round the edge of the display. Staple the carpet piece, the baby's blanket, the socks, scarf, pom-pom hat, cardigan, slippers and gloves all around the central sheep. Using strands of wool the same colour as the sheep, connect each item to the sheep. Label the display 'Wool is warm' and write out labels for all the woollen items. Punch a hole in each label and let the children place them on the hook-pins which have been positioned under each item.

Explore the display with the children, for example let them practise removing and replacing the item labels on the appropriate hooks.

✧ Feel and smell some real sheep's wool before it has been washed.
✧ Position a skein of wool over two chair backs and show how it can be wound into a ball.
✧ Turn a multicoloured knitted garment inside out and see how the different colours weave into each other.
✧ Assemble and mix different lengths, thickness and colours of wool then sort them into sets.

Discussion

In winter, sheep need thick woolly coats to keep them warm. In summer when they want to be cooler, they have their coats cut short – just like when we have our hair cut. What happens to their wool before we can use it? What do we make from clean sheep's wool?

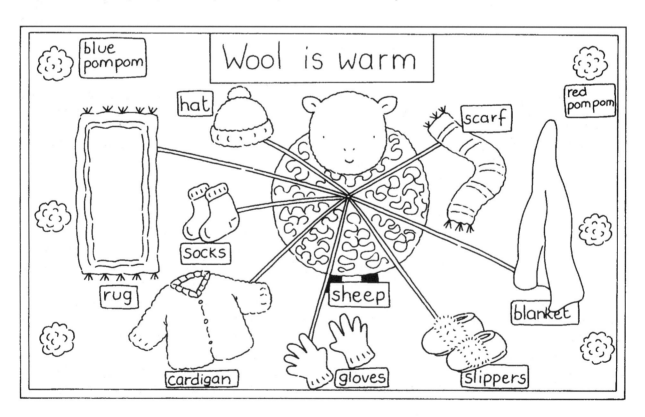

COLLECTING HOBBIES

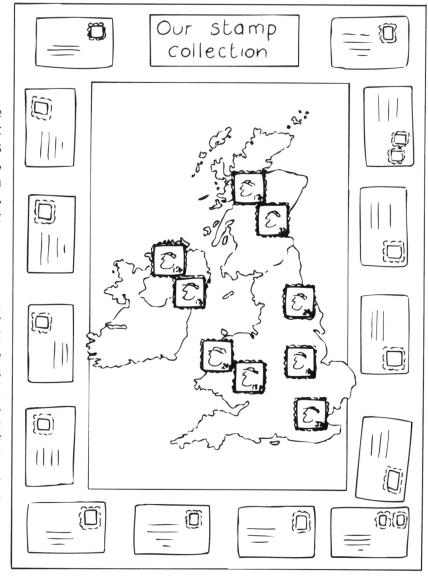

What you need

Frieze paper, a large clear outline map of the British Isles (at least A3 size). Plenty of envelopes with used British stamps on, scissors, shallow dishes, water, a cookery timer, paper towels, adhesive sticks, stapler, labelling card and pens.

What to do

Staple the map of the British Isles to the frieze-lined display area. Let the children handle all the envelopes looking at the stamps carefully for similarities and differences. Cut the used stamps off some envelopes leaving plenty of margin. Float the cut stamps in the bowl of shallow water — like little ships! Set the timer for twenty minutes and then peel the stamps carefully off their backing paper. The stamps should still be sticky enough to attach directly onto the map in the appropriate places, for example those with a symbol of a lion are from Scotland; those with the symbol of a dragon come from Wales; those with the red hand of Ulster are from Ireland; those with only the Queen's head are from England.

If the stamps have lost their stickiness (were immersed in the water or were left soaking for too long) leave them to dry on a paper towel and then fix them in place with the adhesive stick. Frame the display area with other used envelopes. Label the display 'Our stamp collection'.

Follow up the display work by:
✧ showing the children a newly-stamped envelope and comparing it to one that has been sent through the post. How can you tell the difference? (By looking at the franking marks.)
✧ looking at some commemorative stamps which can be bought from Post Offices and seeing if you can recognize any of the animals, people or places

✧ making a writing pattern like the edge of a stamp
✧ finding out where foreign stamps come from on a map of the world
✧ talking about other hobbies which the children might have.

Discussion

During winter the weather can be too cold to go out to play. This is a good time to spend on hobbies such as collecting stamps. Why do we need to put stamps on letters? When stamps were first invented (1840) it cost just one penny to send a letter. The first Penny Black stamps are now famous. In those days, each stamp had to be cut out before it was stuck because there were no perforations. Our Queen's head is on all British stamps. Where do we post letters and buy stamps?

OVER-WINTERING

What you need

A large shallow box, black, brown or pale green sugar paper, dried twigs, leaves, bark and flower heads, sprigs of evergreen plants such as laurel, hay (from a pet shop), adhesive tape, Plasticine, a piece of florist's foam in a plastic carton, a foil plate, two small plantpots, some pebbles, small balls of damp clay, cocktail sticks, florist's wire, shoelaces, different coloured paints and brushes, a black marker pen and labelling card.

ladybirds, dormice, frogs, worms and slugs. Use the cocktail sticks to make the hedgehogs' spikes, florist's wire to make the ladybirds' legs and pieces of shoelace for the dormice's tails.

Paint the clay creatures when they are dry and draw on any spots or features with the black marker pen. Hide the creatures in the winter scene. Label your display 'Find where the creatures are spending winter'.

Let the children use the display by taking turns to hide the creatures in different places in the box and seeing if their friends can find them all.

Follow up the display work by:

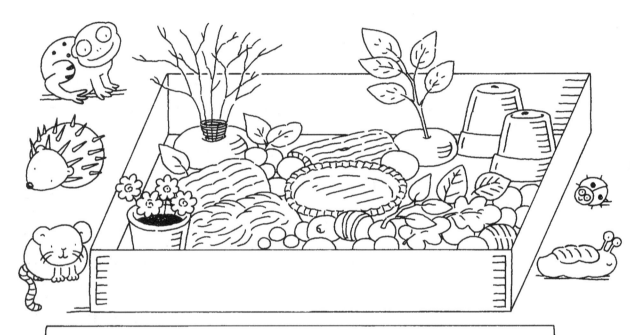

Find where the creatures are spending winter.

What to do

Cover the inside and outside of a shallow box with the sugar paper. Gather the twigs and tape them together to look like a bare winter tree. Push the 'trunk' firmly into the piece of Plasticine and press this into the base of the box.

Do the same with the laurel branch. Push the dried flower heads into the carton containing the florist's foam and stick in place. Place the foil plate into the box to look like a pond and arrange dried leaves, bark, pebbles and hay around it and across the base of the box.

Turn the plantpots upside down and put them in a corner. Pinch, pull, roll and mould the clay to make hiding winter creatures such as hedgehogs,

✧ sorting the creatures into groups and then labelling them — which set has the most creatures?
✧ comparing the shape of slugs and worms — which one is the fattest?

Discussion

Some animals hibernate over winter (see 'Make a den' on page 38) but others just hide among the leaves, tree roots and dried stems of plants in the garden. Which creatures come inside the house to hide from the winter cold? (Spiders, lacewings, butterflies and flies.) Where do some birds spend the winter? (See 'A winter holiday' on page 37.) If you had to spend winter outside where would you choose to hide?

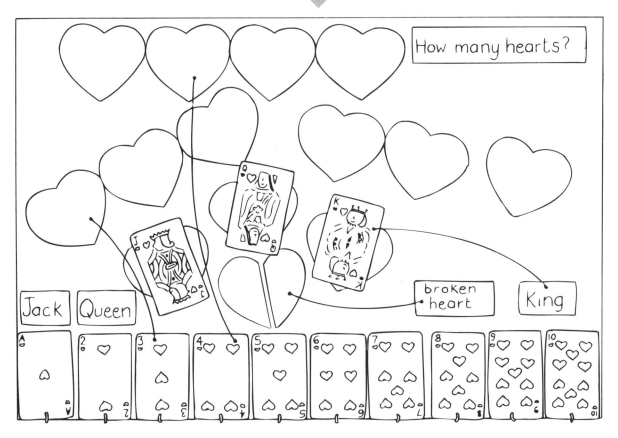

VALENTINE HEARTS

What you need

Pink frieze paper to line the display area, eight pieces of red A4 paper, a pencil, scissors, a hole punch, a stapler, PVA adhesive and spreader, adhesive tape, the 13 heart cards from an old pack of playing cards, labelling card and a black marker pen, 14 shoelaces (or string with a paperclip tied to the end), Blu-Tack.

What to do

Fold and cut a sheet of red paper in half lengthways to make two long strips. Fold each strip into eighths then refold the strips along the creases to form concertinas (see diagram). Hold all the folded edges tightly together and draw half a heart shape on the top fold so that it touches both edges. Cut round the half heart but leave a little on the left folds intact. Open up the strip to see four joined complete hearts. Repeat this with five more sheets of paper. Cut or join the concertinas where necessary, to make nine groups of hearts starting with one on its own and building up to nine. Make four big separate hearts in the same way from two whole sheets of paper folded into quarters. Stick the King, Queen and Jack playing cards onto each big heart and cut the remaining big heart in half. Write onto four labelling cards: King, Queen, Jack, Broken Heart.

Punch a hole in the bottom of the labels and the rest of the heart playing cards. Tie a lace through each hole and staple all the cards across the bottom of the display area. Staple the big hearts and the concertinas randomly above the cards so that the folds are slightly raised. Press some Blu-Tack underneath each group of hearts so that the laces can be held in position later. Label the display 'How many hearts?'

See if the children can match up the laces from the playing cards to the appropriate number of hearts or picture cards and press the lace into the Blu-Tack. Follow up the display work by making some heart-shaped biscuits and decorating them with silver balls; run around very fast and then feel your heart racing.

Discussion

A heart is the symbol of love. If a person is upset that someone they love doesn't love them, we say that they are 'broken-hearted'. The heart you have inside you is used to pump your blood around your body to keep you fit and healthy.

CHAPTER 8
ASSEMBLIES

The assemblies in this chapter focus on the ideas of helping ourselves, helping others and not being afraid to ask for help during the winter months.

MAKING DO

The purpose of this gathering together is to give the children the idea that people are able to adapt to circumstances however difficult, and that with thought and imagination they can use whatever resources are available to make life easier for everyone.

up and down pretend stairs, or playing chase around the furniture). The householders would not be able to go out to the shops either, and if they had run out of some foods they might have to make do with peculiar meals such as eating spaghetti with chocolate sprinkled on it! Ask the children if they can suggest some funny food combinations.

Introduction

Tell the children the Aesop's fable about the thirsty crow who spotted a jug with water in it. He flew down immediately to have a drink only to find that he couldn't get his beak far enough into the jug to reach the water. He tried in every way to get at the water and was about to give up when he noticed there were some pebbles nearby. He dropped the pebbles into the jug until the water level rose high enough for him to have his drink. Demonstrate this principle to the children.

Activity

Ask the children to imagine a situation where they are snowed in at home (see 'Snowed in' page 30). Explain that they may not be able to do all the things they normally do, for example they might not be able to take the dog outside for its walk.

Ask for volunteers to show how the dog could have its exercise around the house (perhaps running

Reflection

Sometimes things go wrong in our lives and when this happens, if we think hard and experiment, we can often find ways to cope.

The crow found a way to reach the water in the jug and have a drink. The children found ways to exercise their imaginary dog during bad winter weather and they were able to think of strange food combinations which they could eat.

Prayer

Please let us remember that even if we are snowed in we must not give up and that we can find a way to manage through our difficulties.

Song

Sing the song 'There's A Hole In My Bucket' from *Apusskidu* (A & C Black).

HELPING OUT

During this assembly the children will be able to think about ways in which they can help other people. Understanding the needs of others is a gift in itself.

Introduction

Have any of the children ever moved house or had some new neighbours move into the house next door to them. Did they notice what a busy time it was and how difficult it was to find the things that were needed among all the packing cases? Ask the children to think about meeting a family of new neighbours who have come from a hot country and have arrived here in the middle of winter. What will they need?

Activity

Collect the following items and put them into a box or basket: a winter coat, a woolly hat, thick socks, wellingtons, an umbrella, a blanket, a hot water bottle, a toy tea tray set for tea, enough small pieces of cake for the whole group. Select four children to wait in the play house as if they are the new neighbours. Ask another child to choose an item from the box, then to knock at the play house door and welcome the new people by giving them an item. Encourage the child to explain to the newcomers why the item will be needed – for example, 'I have brought you this hot water bottle to keep your feet warm in bed'. Let the other children give the remaining things from the box.

Finish with everybody sitting together and sharing the cake.

Reflection

Think about how difficult it is to move from a familiar place to somewhere that is strange. This move could be from home to school, or from one house to another or even from one country to another. Consider how comforting it would be that someone is willing to lend you their things especially when you came from a warm place to somewhere that is wintry and cold.

Prayer

Let us be thankful that we have enough warm clothes and food to be able to share them with other people, especially those who have never experienced the cold weather of our winter.

Song

Sing the song 'When I Needed A Neighbour' *Someone's Singing Lord* (A & C Black).

ASKING FOR HELP

This assembly discusses the idea that we cannot do everything for ourselves. Sometimes we need to enlist the help of others who are ready and willing to help.

Introduction

When sheep graze (eat) in the hills and fields it looks as if they do not belong to anyone. However, each farmer knows which are his/her own sheep because they are marked with different colours or numbers using a special spray paint. Discuss what happens when snow falls very thickly (see 'Footprints in the snow' on page 18 and 'Saint Bernard' on page 39) and what might happen to the sheep in the fields (they would be buried under the snow). Tell the children that you want them to act out a scene of sheep which are lost in snow.

Activity

Ask for some volunteers to pretend to be sheep grazing in the fields before the bad weather starts. Wearing socks on their hands, encourage them to pad round the room on all fours, munching away at the grass and pulling at a few remaining leaves left on hedges and trees. Suddenly it starts to snow — ask some children to stand at the sides fluttering their fingers as if snow is falling. The 'sheep' start to huddle together as the snow gets thicker and thicker — lay a white sheet over the top of the 'sheep' who are now hidden by the thick snow. A child farmer comes along with his sheep-dog (another child) and a bale of hay (a box) looking for his sheep. When he can't see them he sets his 'dog' to sniff all over the room until it finds where the sheep are buried in the deep snow. The 'farmer' now helps the sheep out of the snow (removes the sheet), feeds them with hay and thanks his dog for the help.

Reflection

Let us realize we cannot do everything on our own — sometimes we need the help of others and we should never be frightened to ask for this help.

Prayer

Please let us know when to ask for help especially if we need it during cold winter weather.

Song

Sing 'See How The Snowflakes Are Falling' from *Someone's Singing Lord* (A & C Black).

Collective worship in schools

The assemblies outlined here are suitable for use with children in nurseries and playgroups, but would need to be adapted for use with pupils at registered schools. As a result of legislation enacted in 1944, 1988 and 1993, there are now specific points to be observed when developing a programme of Collective Acts of Worship in a school.

Further guidance will be available from your local SACRE — Standing Advisory Council for RE.

POEMS AND ACTION RHYMES

WRAP UP!

'Put on your scarf
Your gloves and your hat.
Do up your buttons.
Come here, not like that!'

Mum wraps me up
Like a parcel to post,
So I hardly can move,
But I'm warm as toast!!

Barbara Garrad

WINTER FRIEND

I made a brand new friend today
            He's very tall.
We played outside together all day
            Beside the wall.
The snowball fights were won by me
            He didn't care.
I didn't ask him in for tea
            He waited there.
I let him borrow my best scarf
            It made him smile.
And Mummy's hat to make him laugh
            He liked the style!
His eyes are lovely, dark as stone
            They really shine.
An orange nose is his alone
            Not like mine.
I made this friend from out of snow
            I really hope he'll never go.

Brenda Williams

ANYONE BORED?

Crayons, chalks, pencils, pens
Books, comics
Making dens

Dolls, castles, pirates, toys
Games for girls
Or games for boys

Gluing, cutting, sticking things in
Games you lose
And games you win

Felt craft, building, painting things
Wearing hats and
Trying on rings

Sewing, cooking, puzzles and more
Games at the table
Games on the floor

Boats, trains, rockets and cars
Travel games, space games
Flying to Mars

Snakes and ladders, Blindman's Buff
Dominoes, cards and
All that stuff

Indoor games and cake for tea
Anyone bored?
No, not me!

Brenda Williams

WINTER WEATHER

Foggy day
We can't see
Hold on tight
Follow me!

Diamonds on
The window pane
Splashy walks
In the rain

Hail falling
Hard and white
Stay inside
Hail can bite!

Skiddy roads
Ice in sheets
Slippy steps
Frozen feet

Silent world
Soft and white
Snow has fallen
In the night

Brenda Williams

IT'S SNOWED

It's snowed! It's snowed!
It's blocked the road.
The school is closed today!
Come on! Come on!
Get your wellies on!
We're going out to play.

We'll stamp footprints
In the snow
To show where we have been.
We'll build a snowman
In the park
Down beside the stream.

We'll get the sledge
Out of the shed
And go up by the mill.
We'll sit upright
And cling on tight
As we hurtle down the hill.

We'll roll about.
We'll laugh and shout,
And make snowballs to throw.
Come on! Come on!
Get your anorak on!
Come and play in the snow.

John Foster

SNOW STAMPING

(an action rhyme)

Sometimes the snowflakes
fall from the sky.
  (make fluttery downward movements with fingers, high to low)

They look like a carpet,
so smoothly they lie.
  (spread open hands outwards over imaginary smooth surface)

I put on my wellies,
then here's how I go...
  (mime pulling on both boots, then prepare for action...)

stamping my footprints
right into the snow.
  (stamp footsteps out firmly in time to the rhythm of the
  words, 'on <u>stamp</u>ing', '<u>foot</u>prints', '<u>into</u>' and '<u>snow</u>' ...
  4 heavy, stepped stamps, or on the spot if preferred)

Tony Mitton

Here comes the robin

ROBIN RHYME

(an action rhyme)

Here comes the robin,
bobbing on the sill.
(make sill with horizontal arm / make robin with
hand of other arm formed into beak shape / bob
this hand along the sill in time with the words)

He cocks his head
and he pecks with his bill.
(show these two actions with the robin-hand / one
cock of head, three pecks with bill, on words 'pecks',
'with' and 'bill', in rhythm with verse)

Set out some water.
(mime this / place saucer on horizontal arm)

Sprinkle some seed.
(mime this with thumb and fingers over
horizontal arm)

That's what a robin
(make robin on sill again)
in winter will need.
(3 pecks again, on last 3 words, in rhythm)

Tony Mitton

REINDEER

Far, far away
the reindeer live
in a land of ice
and snow...

When it's nearly
Christmas,
I wonder if
they know?

Nuzzling around
for a nibble of moss
in the freezing, arctic
day —

Do they guess
there's a sledge to pull
miles and miles
away?

Under a wide
star-sprinkled sky
that's shining
winter-bright,

Father Christmas
is loading up...
ready
for Christmas night!

Jean Kenward

A PUZZLE – WHAT AM I?

I'm standing in a garden
Holding up my hands.
The snow is falling gently
I listen while it lands.

I'm very tall and very green
Even in this snow.
My leaves won't fall down on the ground
I'm evergreen, you know!

But when the time for Christmas comes
The people look at me.
They dig my roots and pull me up
To be their...WHAT AM I?
I'm the family Christmas Tree!

Stevie Ann Wilde

LOG FIRE

Feel the warmth
spread across your cheek,

listen to the logs
crackle and creak.

Watch the flames
make a flickering light,

smell the air —
what's cooking tonight?

Taste those chestnuts —
let's have a bite!

Tracey Blance

PHOTOCOPIABLE RESOURCES

WINTER SEEDS

All among the leaf litter
lie the winter seeds,
acorns, beech nuts, conkers, berries;
seeds from garden weeds.

All the long, cold winter
through frost, hail, sleet and snow,
seeds wait, nestling near the earth,
for the time when they can grow.

Penny Kent

HIBERNATING HEDGEHOG

Here comes Winter,
cold and grey.
It's time to tuck
myself away.

Here comes ice
and here comes snow.
I need somewhere
warm to go.

Here comes mist
and freezing fog.
Here's a good old
hollow log.

And here's a pile
of leaves that's deep.
I'll roll up here
and go to sleep.

Tony Mitton

I'VE MADE A STAR

I've made a star
And pretty things
And bought a doll
With angel wings.

Silver tinsel
Baubles bright
Some tinkling bells
And coloured lights.

We've wooden toys
And tiny treats
Christmas crackers
And little sweets

So now we're off
To fetch our tree
Then Christmas time
Is here for me!

Brenda Williams

MY TREASURE

Down in the garden
Where only I have been
There is a treasure
No one else has seen

Deep, deeply buried
Some time ago
Soon all was covered
By white crispy snow

Soon, though it's winter
When I look near the tree
My treasure will be showing
But only I shall see

Tiny spears of green stems
Shiny pearly tops
These are my treasure
My own snowdrops

Brenda Williams

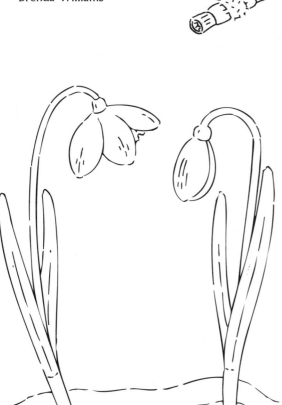

STORIES

THE WINTER HEDGEHOG

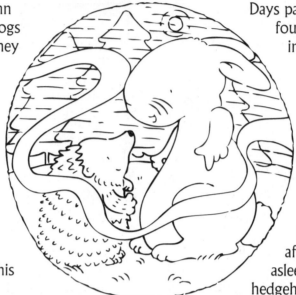

One cold, misty autumn afternoon, the hedgehogs gathered in a wood. They were searching the undergrowth for leaves for their nests, preparing for the long sleep of winter.

All that is, except one.

The smallest hedgehog overheard two foxes talking about winter. 'What is winter?' he had asked his mother.

'Winter comes when we are asleep,' she had replied. 'It can be beautiful, but it can also be dangerous, cruel and very, very cold. It's not for the likes of us. Now go to sleep.'

But the smallest hedgehog couldn't sleep. As evening fell he slipped away to look for winter. When hedgehogs are determined they can move very swiftly, and soon the little hedgehog was far away from home. An owl swooped down from high in a tree.

'Hurry home,' he called. 'It's time for your long sleep.' But on and on went the smallest hedgehog until the sky turned dark and the trees were nothing but shadows.

The next morning, the hedgehog awoke to find the countryside covered in fog. 'Who goes there?' called a voice, and a large rabbit emerged from the mist; amazed to see a hedgehog about with winter coming on.

'I'm looking for winter,' replied the hedgehog. 'Can you tell me where it is?'

'Hurry home,' said the rabbit. 'Winter is on its way and it's not time for hedgehogs.'

But the smallest hedgehog wouldn't listen. He was determined to find winter.

Days passed. The little hedgehog found plenty of slugs and insects to eat, but he couldn't find winter anywhere.

Then one day, the air turned icy cold. Birds flew home to their roosts and the animals hid in their burrows and warrens. The smallest hedgehog felt very lonely and afraid and wished he was asleep with the other hedgehogs. But it was too late to turn back now!

That night winter came. A frosty wind swept through the grass and blew the last straggling leaves from the trees. In the morning the whole countryside was covered in a carpet of snow.

'Winter!' said the smallest hedgehog. 'I've found it at last.' And all the birds flew down from the trees to join him.

The trees were completely bare and the snow sparkled on the grass. The little hedgehog went to the river to drink, but it was frozen. He shivered, shook his prickles and stepped on to the ice. His feet began to slide and the faster he scurried, the faster he sped across it. 'Winter is wonderful,' he cried. At first he did not see the fox, like a dark shadow, slinking towards him.

'Hello! Come and join me,' he called as the fox reached the river bank. But the fox only heard the rumble of his empty belly. With one leap he pounced on to the ice. When the little hedgehog saw his sly yellow eyes he understood what the fox was about. But every time he tried to run away he slipped on the ice. He curled into a ball and spiked his prickles.

'Ouch!' cried the fox. The sharp prickles stabbed his paws and he reeled towards the centre of the river where he disappeared beneath the thin ice.

'That was close', the smallest hedgehog cried to himself. 'Winter is beautiful, but it is also cruel, dangerous and very, very cold.'

Winter was everywhere: in the air, in the trees, on the ground and in the hedgerows. Colder and colder it grew until the snow froze under the hedgehog's feet. Then the snow came again and a cruel north wind picked it up and whipped it into a blizzard. The night fell as black as ink and he lost his way. 'Winter is dangerous and cruel and very, very cold,' moaned the little hedgehog.

Luck saved him. A hare scurrying home gave him shelter in his burrow. By morning the snow was still falling, but gently now, covering everything it touched in a soft white blanket.

The smallest hedgehog was enchanted as he watched the pattern his paws made. Reaching the top of a hill, he rolled into a ball and spun over and over, turning himself into a great white snowball as he went. Down and down he rolled until he reached the feet of two children building a snowman.

'Hey, look at this,' said the little girl, 'a perfect head for our snowman.'

'I'm a hedgehog,' he cried. But no one heard his tiny hedgehog voice.

The girl placed the hedgehog snowball on the snowman's body and the boy used a carrot for a nose and pebbles for the eyes. 'Let me out,' shouted the hedgehog. But the children just stood back and admired their work before going home for lunch.

When the children had gone, the cold and hungry hedgehog nibbled at the carrot nose. As he munched, the sun came out and the snow began to melt. He blinked in the bright sunlight, tumbled down the snowman's body and was free.

Time went on. The hedgehog saw the world in its winter cloak. He saw bright red berries disappear from the hedgerows as the birds collected them for their winter larders. And he watched the children speed down the hill on their sleighs.

The winter passed. One day the air grew warmer and the river began to flow again. A stoat, who had changed his coat to winter white, changed it back to brown. Then the little hedgehog found crocuses and snowdrops beneath the trees and he knew it was time to go home. Slowly he made his way back to the wood.

From out of every log, sleepy hedgehogs were emerging from their long sleep.

'Where have you been?' they called to the smallest hedgehog.

'I found winter,' he replied.

'And what was it like?' asked his mother.

'It was wonderful and beautiful, but it was also...'

'Dangerous, cruel and very, very cold,' finished his mother.

But she was answered by a yawn, a sigh and a snore and the smallest hedgehog was fast asleep.

Ann and Reg Cartwright

PHOTOCOPIABLE RESOURCES

THE SNOW WHALE

One November night, snow fell fast and thick as down from a duck's back. In the morning, the hills were hump-backed with snow.

Laurie ran into the garden and searched for a stick. She drew a great shape in the hillside. Her little brother, Leo, ploughed through the snow after her, holding high his bucket and spade.

'What shall I do?' he asked.

'Pile up the snow,' she said.

'What are you building?'

'A whale.'

'Where does the snow come from?' asked Leo.

His sister sighed. 'Don't you know *anything*?' she said. 'The water rises up from the sea and goes into the clouds. Sometimes it comes down again as snow.'

Out ran Rory from next door. He brought his wheelbarrow to help, and his sister Kate brought a garden rake.

'Where will the whale swim?' asked Leo.

Nobody answered. They were too busy huffing and puffing, bringing the whale out of the hill.

'Fetch me the rake, Leo,' said Laurie.

'Why?'

'To draw his tail flukes and his big filter mouth.'

'But what will he eat?' asked Leo.

Nobody answered, so he brought her the rake.

'Fetch me Dad's ladder, Leo,' said Laurie.

'Why?'

'To climb up his back and make his blow-hole.'

'What will he blow?' asked Leo.

Nobody answered, so he brought her the ladder. On the way back, he found a special stone on the path.

'Here's the whale's eye!' he cried.

'It's very tiny,' said Laurie.

'But it looks happy,' said Leo, and he climbed up to put it on the whale's face.

They shovelled and dug and bucketed and wheeled and packed and patted and polished and smoothed. Then they stood back and looked.

He was the most beautiful snow whale in the whole world: high as a church, round as a cloud, white as an ice-floe.

In the afternoon the whale looked blue.

'That's because he's freezing,' said Laurie, 'and so am I.'

They ran home to thaw their fingers and dry their gloves and socks, and to eat hot toast and cake.

As darkness settled over the hillside, Laurie and Leo watched the whale from their window.

'The valley's just a jam-jar to him,' said Laurie. 'If he sang, his voice would shatter the hills. If he thrashed his tail, he would break our house in two.'

Next day, it was so cold that the snow whale's mouth was full of icicles. The children played with him all day. They ran round him, climbed on his back and slid down his sides. They sailed him over the seven seas. They told him stories about ants and elephants and made him smile.

Later, when the sun broke through and water drops dripped from the branches, the snow whale glistened like silver.

'Where does the snow go?' asked Leo.

His sister sighed.

'Don't you know *anything*?' she said. 'It melts and flows back into the rivers and down into the seas again.'

That night, Leo dreamed of whales singing in the hills and playing with their calves at the bottom of the sea.

When he woke, someone was crying, but it wasn't the whale. It was Laurie.

'Where has the whale gone?' she sobbed.

'I *do* know that,' Leo said, and put his arms round her. 'He's gone back to the sea again. Snow Whale's gone home.'

Caroline Pitcher

BIANCA'S WINTER COAT

'We're going shopping today to buy new coats for the winter,' Mum told Bianca and Josh, one morning.

'Good!' said Josh. He liked going shopping. 'Can Panda have a new coat, too?' A threadbare toy panda dangled from Josh's hand.

'I'm sure Gran will be pleased to knit him one,' said Mum, tying Josh's shoelaces for him.

'I like my *old* coat,' said Bianca. 'I don't want a new one!'

Bianca loved her orange anorak with big yellow spots. It was bright and cheerful to wear.

'It's too small and shabby now,' Mum told her. 'And anyway, it won't keep out the cold. It's not warm enough, Bianca.'

'No, no, no!' shouted Bianca. She ran to fetch her coat and put it on. 'See, it fits just right,' she said. 'And it keeps me warm and dry. I don't need a new one.'

'Just as you like,' said Mum. 'Josh and I will have new coats then. Now, come on. I want to be back for lunch.'

It was a particularly cold day so they wrapped up warmly with gloves and scarves and set off for the shops. Bianca pulled her orange coat closer around her. The buttons kept popping open so she had to hold it together, but the cold wind still felt as if it was blowing right through.

They looked for a coat for Josh first. It wasn't difficult. Josh immediately spotted a fleecy green duffel coat with a friendly-looking dragon on the front. He grabbed it as soon as he saw it.

'Want this one!' he said firmly.

'Let's try it on then, and make sure it fits,' said Mum. She had a quick look at the price tag to make sure it wasn't too expensive.

The coat was perfect. Josh looked at his reflection in the mirror and held up Panda. 'See – Panda likes it too!' he grinned.

Bianca looked at herself in the mirror. She noticed that the sleeves of her jumper were showing beneath the sleeves of her coat. Frowning, she tucked them up.

Josh liked his new coat so much he wouldn't take it off.

Mum laughed and asked the shop assistant to take off the tickets and put Josh's old coat in a bag instead.

'Now we'll go and find one for me,' said Mum.

Mum took ages choosing her coat. She tried on a great many different ones before she finally found one she liked.

'This is smart and warm,' she said, looking at her reflection in the mirror. 'Do you like it, Bianca?'

'You look very nice,' Bianca admitted.

Josh looked at himself and Panda in the mirror, too. So did Bianca. Then she noticed that her anorak looked very short. Frowning, she tugged it down over her skirt.

Mum wanted to wear her new coat, too, so the shop assistant took all the tickets off it and put her old coat in a bag for her.

'That's that then,' said Mum. 'Let's go home.'

Mum and Josh looked really smart in their new coats. Bianca began to wish she had a new coat, after all.

'I suppose I could just *look* at the coats before we go,' she said. 'I might see something I like.'

'Good idea,' agreed Mum. 'It doesn't hurt to look.'

Winter coats seemed to come in all different colours and wonderful fabrics: quilted, furry, fleecy and woolly. Bianca hardly knew where to start. Then a bright red, woollen coat with yellow toggles and sunflowers stitched on the pockets caught

Bianca's eye. She held it up and looked at it. It was *very* pretty.

'Do you want to try it on?' asked Mum.

'Um, yes please.'

Bianca slipped on the coat and went over to the mirror. She twirled around. The coat fitted her perfectly. Inside it was lined with a warm, quilted material, and it had a hood which buttoned under her chin to keep out the wind and rain. It was lovely. Much better than her old anorak. Mum was right, that *was* getting a bit shabby and small, and it wasn't much good in winter weather.

'Nice,' said Josh. Panda nodded his head, with a bit of help from Josh. 'Panda says it's nice, too.'

'Very pretty,' said Mum. 'Do you want it?'

'Yes, please,' Bianca nodded eagerly. 'Can I wear it now?'

'Of course,' smiled Mum.

So the shop assistant took off the shop tickets and put Bianca's old coat in a bag for her. Then they all went home, wearing their new winter coats.

'Well,' laughed Mum. 'This is the first time I've come back from a shopping trip with bags full of *old* clothes!'

Karen King

SONGS

THE WINTER WEATHER BAND

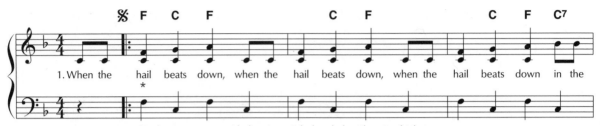

1. When the hail beats down, when the hail beats down, when the hail beats down in the

Each verse repeats with the piano right hand played an 8va higher.
Percussion, playing straight crotchets, is added and the vocal line omitted.

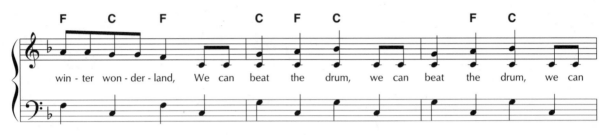

win-ter won-der-land, We can beat the drum, we can beat the drum, we can

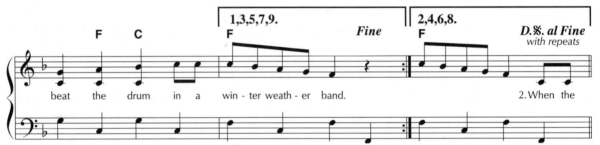

1,3,5,7,9.   *Fine*   2,4,6,8.   *D.%. al Fine*
with repeats

beat the drum in a win-ter weath-er band.   2. When the

2. When the wind shakes the trees...
We can shake our tambourines... [tambourine plays in repeat]

3. When the sun comes out...
We can ring our bells... [Indian bells play in repeat]

4. When the ice goes drip...
We can tap our claves... [claves play in repeat]

Ann Bryant

SNOWFLAKES

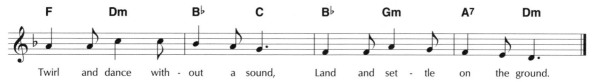

Sue Nicholls

FIVE FRIENDLY SNOWMEN

2. Four ... three.
3. Three ... two.
4. Two ... was one friendly snowman.
5. One ... snowman ... no ... .

Pat Sweet

LITTLE FOOTPRINTS

One lit-tle foot step, Two lit-tle foot steps, three lit-tle foot steps, four. Who put foot steps

in the snow when there weren't an-y steps be-fore? One lit-tle foot step, two lit-tle foot steps,

Miss this section out 1st time, then as children add their own ideas repeat as often as necessary

three lit-tle foot steps four. Was it a —— or was it a ——?

Was it a bird or was it a cat? Or was it the dog next door?

Clive Barnwell

BOBBLE HAT

I need a hat to wear in the win - ter. I need a hat to keep me warm.

I need a hat to wear in the win - ter, Some - thing to keep my cold head warm

*Chorus**

Bob - ble hat, bob - ble hat, bob - ble, bob - ble, bob - ble hat. Bob - ble hat, bob - ble hat, keep me warm.
Flop - py hat, flop - py hat, flop - py, flop - py, flop - py hat.

Bob - ble hat, bob - ble hat, bob - ble, bob - ble, bob - ble hat, save me from the rain, from the snow and from the storm.

*Different hats, such as a baseball hat, or even a bowler hat can be used in the Chorus

Clive Barnwell

A HAPPY NEW YEAR TO YOU

Slowly

We wave good-bye to the old. We say hel-lo to the new. We

sing, our song and wish ev'-ry-one A hap-py new year to you. We

hap-py new year to you. A hap-py new year to you.

Johanne Levy

CANDLELIGHT

Let's make a hol - der for a can - dle, Let's make the hol - der look just right.

We'll draw a plan then match it if we can then We'll light the can - dle,

bright flick' - ring can - dle, send - ing out its spec - ial can - dle - light.

Peter Morrell

FOOTPRINTS IN THE SNOW

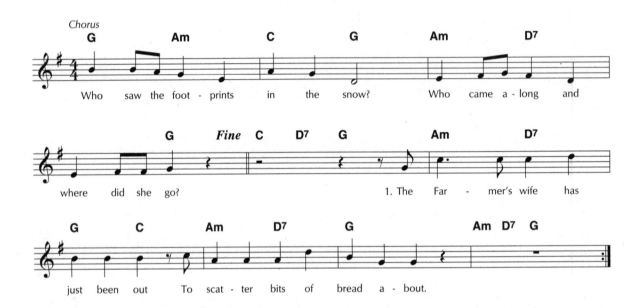

Chorus
G | Am | C | G | Am | D7
Who saw the foot - prints in the snow? Who came a - long and

G | Fine C D7 G | Am | D7
where did she go? 1. The Far - mer's wife has

G | C | Am | D7 | G | Am D7 G
just been out To scat - ter bits of bread a - bout.

2. One little sparrow was out today,
He ate some bread and hopped away ... *chorus*

3. A pigeon ate some breadcrumbs too,
He walked around, then off he flew ... *chorus*

4. A cat crept up behind the hedge,
Then sprang on to the window ledge ... *chorus*

5. A squirrel found the snow too deep,
So went off home to have some sleep ... *chorus*

6. On his horse, the farmer's son,
Went riding off to have some fun.

Jan Betts

AULD LANG SYNE

Words: Robert Burns

This version by Jenny Morris

THEMES
for early years

Name _____

Winter words

skis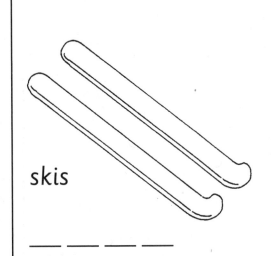

_ _ _ _

snowman

_ _ _ _ _ _ _

smoke

_ _ _ _ _

 skates

_ _ _ _ _ _

sledge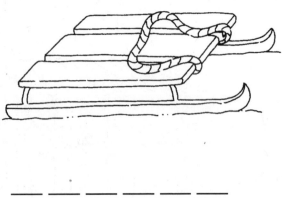

_ _ _ _ _ _

scarf

_ _ _ _ _

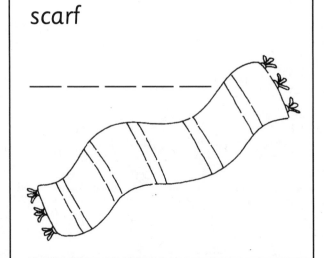

Follow the prints

Start your pencil at the bread dish and follow the footprints to find out who made them.

THEMES
for early years

Name _____

Hot and cold clothes

Colour the clothes worn in hot weather – red.
Colour the clothes worn in cold weather – blue.

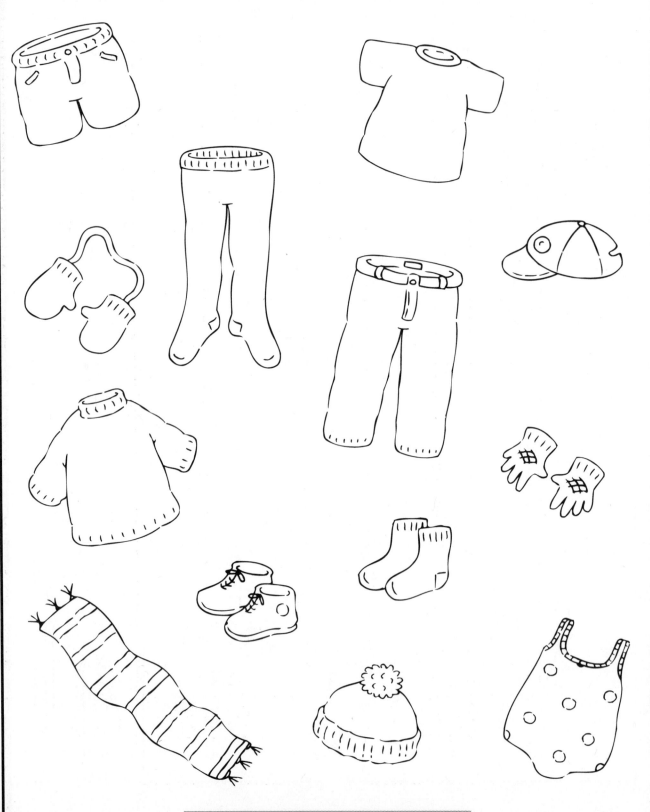

Name _____

Measure the temperature
Colour inside the bulb and tube to the correct level.

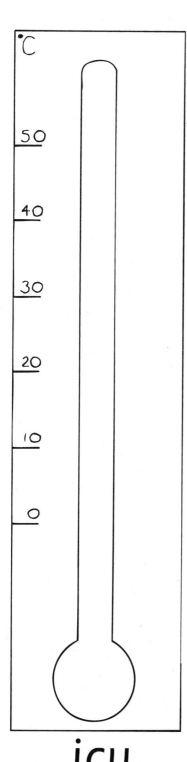

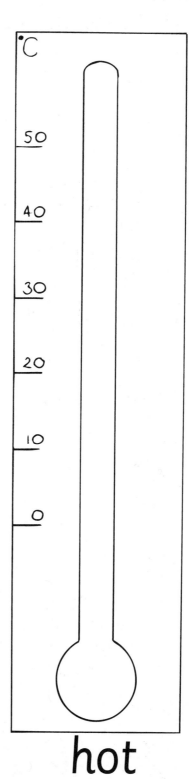

icy

hot

_____   _____

THEMES
for early years

Name _____

A winter's day

Use a white crayon to show where light snow would land. Cut along the dotted lines to make jigsaw pieces.

THEMES
for early years

Name _____

The acorn game

Finish

Start→

THEMES
for early years

Name _____

A different note

Draw a ring round the one which is different on each line. Now make all the notes in the row look the same.

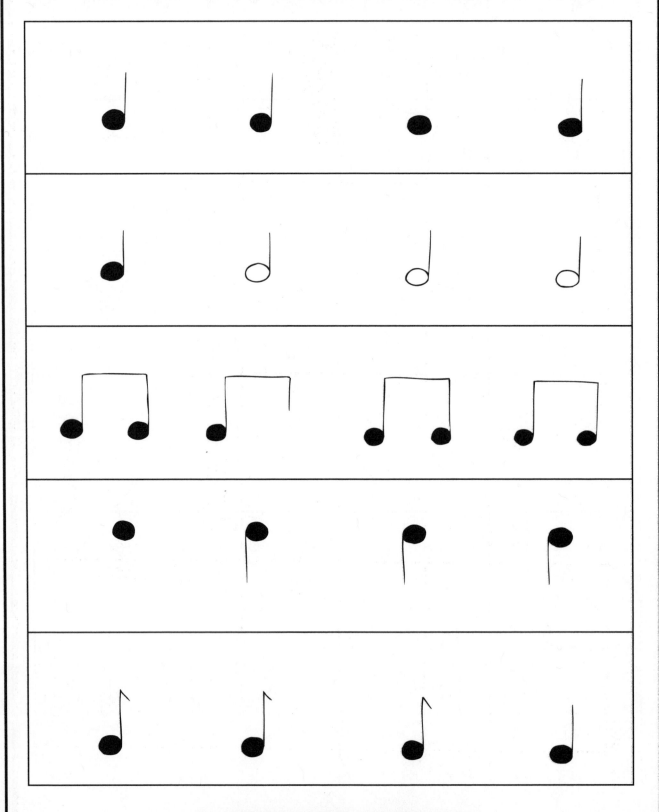

Name _____

Make a box

RECOMMENDED RESOURCES

INFORMATION BOOKS

Adults' Encyclopaedia Britannica (Encyclopaedia Britannica)
Children's Encyclopaedia Britannica (Encyclopaedia Britannica)
'Clothes and Fashion' Joanne Jessop *Looking Back* series (Wayland)
Big Book of Baby Animals (Dorling Kindersley)
'Dogs' *Collins Gems* (Harper Collins)
'Birds' *Collins Gems* (Harper Collins)
The Visual Dictionary of Animals (Dorling Kindersley)
Plants and Flowers – Gardeners' Encyclopaedia The Royal Horticultural Society (Dorling Kindersley)
'Trees' *Eye Witness Explorers* Linda Gamlin (Dorling Kindersley)
'Insects' *Eye Witness Explorers* Steve Parker (Dorling Kindersley)

PICTURE BOOKS AND STORY BOOKS

Water Babies Charles Kingsley (Puffin)
'The Enormous Turnip' *Traditional Story Activities* Jenny Morris (Scholastic)
First Snow Kim Lewis (Walker Books)
The Shepherd Boy Kim Lewis (Walker Books)
Penguin Small Mick Inkpen (Hodder)
Ridiculous! Michael Coleman (Magi Publications)
'The Hare and the Tortoise' *Aesop's Fables* retold by Jacqueline Morley (Macdonald)

OTHER RESOURCES AND USEFUL ADDRESSES

'A Tree for all Seasons' – cloth model with detachable felt pieces from Heron Educational Ltd, Carrwood House, Carrwood Road, Chesterfield S41 9QB. Tel: 01246 453354
'The Four Seasons Framed Puzzles' – four 8-piece wooden puzzles from Hope Education, Orb Mills, Huddersfield, Waterhead, Oldham OL4 2ST. Tel: 0161 628 2788
'Window Decoration Snowstorm' for display purposes from Hope Education (address as above).
'Four Layers Seasons Tree Jigsaw' from NES Arnold, Ludlow Hill Road, West Bridgford, Nottingham NG2 6HD. Tel 0115 971 7700
'All About Weather and Seasons' CD-ROM for PC and Mac from Granada Learning Ltd – SEMEREC Granada Television, Quay Street, Manchester, M60 9EA. Tel: 0161 827 2887.
Polarshield Emergency Blanket obtainable from camping equipment shops.
Royal National Institute for the Blind, 224 Great Portland Street, London WIN 6AA. Tel 0171 388 1266.
Royal National Institute for Deaf People, 19–23 Featherstone Street, London EC1Y 8SL. Tel 0171 296 8000.
The Royal Society for the Protection of Birds, The Lodge, Sandy, Bedfordshire SG19 2DL. Tel 01767 680551.

MUSIC AND SONGS

Apusskidu (A & C Black)
Someone's Singing Lord (A & C Black)
'Seasons: Songs for 4–7 year-olds' *Songbirds* series (A & C Black)
Knock At The Door: Favourite Songs and Rhymes for Young Children Jan Betts (Ward Lock Educational)

POEMS AND RHYMES

This Little Puffin... compiled by Elizabeth Matterson (Puffin)
Book of a Thousand Poems (Harper Collins)
The Oxford Nursery Rhyme Book assembled by Iona and Peter Opie (OUP)
Snow Poems compiled by John Foster (OUP)

PHOTOCOPIABLE RESOURCES